Acknowledgements

P9-APX-946

Spring Flowers: A Harrowsmith Gardener's Guide represents, in its finished state, the commitment and cooperation of many individuals. They include art director Linda Menyes; artist Marta Scythes, who prepared the botanical sketches; senior editor Jennifer Bennett; assistant editor Mary Patton; photo researcher Jane Good; typesetter Patricia Denard-Hinch; production manager Susan Dickinson; copy editor Catherine De Lury and associates Audrey Beard, Sara Perks, Christine Kulyk and Peggy Denard; associate publisher Frank B. Edwards; associate editor Tracy C. Read; and administrative assistant Mirielle Keeling.

Special acknowledgement is extended to the Netherlands Bulb Information Centre, Toronto, Ontario, for its generous assistance in supplying much of the illustrative material from which the artist worked in Chapter Two.

Contents

Introduction

Many readers of *Harrowsmith* magazine have expressed a wish for a book on spring flowers, and it seems natural that this wish should be fulfilled in a series of garden guides which has already focused on ground covers and rock gardens. It also seems natural to look at early flowers not as a collection of individual plants that happen to bloom at the same season of the year but as a harmonious group gathered together into a spring garden. ✑ Four writer-gardeners have collaborated to produce *Spring Flowers: A Harrowsmith Gardener's Guide*. They bring together knowledge and firsthand experience that will get any would-be creator of such a garden off to a good start. ✑ Spring has always been symbolic of new beginnings. For me, this symbolism has real meaning as the early months of 1989 wear away. Left behind in a move last fall was a garden of some five years' standing. Though a long way from being "finished," it had come far enough that each spring was an increasingly heady experience. We welcomed the remembered blooms from the previous year and waited with excitement to see the results of our fall bulb planting. It was the garden where my own apprenticeship began. Now, on a larger farm property, more than enough gardening lies ahead to satisfy even the most obsessive gardener. For this first year, the spring garden will be one 7

Nothing represents the clan of spring-flowering bulbs as well as the modest and pretty crocus, one of the first flowers of a season that ends in June.

of endless discovery in the surrounding woods, coming to life without the help of a gardener's trowel – a special place even after other garden areas begin to demand detailed planning and increasing time and attention. In my own experience, spring – breathtakingly beautiful and all too short – is a time of exhilaration in the garden, a time of giddiness when high resolutions are made and rarely carried through. *This* year I will be weed-perfect . . . keep a garden journal . . . start a serious photographic record. Unlike New Year's resolutions that are firmly tied to January 1, my spring resolutions arise in an elusive and fleeting moment which has nothing to do with the calendar. I would go along with Elspeth Bradbury, the Maritimer on our panel of four authors, who writes, "Officially, spring starts on March 21, the date of the vernal equinox. In March, inevitably, word arrives from my West Coast friends: the daffodils

are up. I greet the news with a growl – the greenest thing around here is envy. In my mind, the ferment of spring is under way, but in the garden, winter still rules the roost. Spring begins for me on the morning I step outside and notice that the air smells of moist earth, the unmistakable scent of spring, as irresistible to gardeners as the whiff of catnip is to cats."

Each winter-weary gardener, in whatever part of the country, will have her or his own set of indications as to the "when" of spring; the "what" will be determined by geographic location – from the gentle, orderly unfolding of a mild, damp climate to the wild burst of colour and growth elsewhere when a long, hard winter finally lets up. Whether slow or sudden, spring can always be certain of its welcome. For Bradbury, spring's essence is concentrated in one month. "May is tulip time, soon to be lilac time. It is the brief season between too cold and too hot – after the

Wildflowers such as trilliums now grow in many spring gardens, where they add their own distinct kind of beauty: simple, unimproved and elegant.

snow flies and before the blackflies. It is the ideal time for gardeners.... Most of us wish the clock would stop for six months one fine morning toward the end of May. But the parade marches on."

If a date on the calendar means little at the beginning of spring, the same is true of spring's departure. The gradual fading into summer will pretty well have taken place before June 21, the summer solstice, and will have been marked in the garden by the ascendance of poppies, peonies and bearded iris. The succeeding seasons will be savoured fully for their own delights, but in the recurring cycle of nature, nothing can be met in the garden with quite the same eagerness and expectation as the miracle of spring.

Katharine Ferguson and her husband recently moved from eastern Ontario to the Bruce Peninsula (Lake Huron/Georgian Bay), where they are planning a commercial gardening venture. Katharine also edited *Rock Gardens: A Harrowsmith Gardener's Guide.*

Chapter One:
Thoughts of Spring

By Elspeth Bradbury

linden tree grows at one end of my garden. A ground cover of lily-of-the-valley thrives at its foot, and primulas and pulmonarias enjoy its summer shade too. By chance, forget-me-nots and violets seeded themselves there. As they often volunteer themselves around the garden, I didn't pay much attention, but I was surprised when scillas and a clump of grape hyacinths also appeared. ✑ "I see you have a spring garden," a visitor commented one May. Apparently I had. ✑ I wasn't about to argue with fate, so I pulled out all the summer flowers and put in violas, white narcissus and a bleeding heart. Now I do indeed have a spring garden, and very pretty it is too, when the linden decks itself in tufts of green and casts a dappled shade over the medley of lemon-yellow, pink, white and innocent blue. By July, of course, the flowers have gone. I used to squeeze in some annual nicotiana, but now I don't. In summer, there is plenty of eye-catching colour elsewhere, and I find this little pool of greenery refreshing. ✑ European writer Karel Čapek described spring as "the rebellious outburst of the will to live." A spring garden may be an acre of woodland, a special corner by the kitchen door or no more than a tub of tulips; but whatever form it takes, it is always the gardener's celebration of that joyful and indomitable spirit, the will to live. ✑ There is nothing like a long winter 11

There is nothing like a long winter to accentuate the beauty of early snowdrops.

to make this gardener appreciate a short spring. In a climate like that of New Brunswick, where I live, the first flowers are the best. I'd trade all my big summer beauties – hollyhocks, day lilies, delphiniums – for a tuft of snowdrops, a scatter of primroses and a sprig of flowering almond. I'd even exchange the glories of autumn for the joys of a spring garden.

Planning

A spring garden begins with an idea, a vision of something beautiful. Most gardeners would like their visions to become instant reality, but beautiful gardens don't happen in a hurry. Take plenty of time to dream and scheme – planning is half the fun. If possible, work with a landscape architect to develop an overall layout for your property. But whether you employ a professional designer or not, do your own research. Read, clip inspiring magazine pictures, look at local gardens and talk to their owners. Ideally, start at least a year ahead, and keep a garden file of notes and sketches throughout the seasons. In summer, it is hard to remember that a snowplough can wreak havoc along the driveway, and in October, who can recall the thrill of daffodils in April?

In planning any garden, there are two main factors to consider: the people and the place.

The People

Northerners try to cram a lot of living into spring and summer, seasons scarcely long enough for all the barbecuing, touring, boating and sunbathing they would like to do, let alone the mowing, clipping, digging and weeding. Gardens are for pleasure, and it isn't any pleasure to be constantly swamped with garden chores. Novice gardeners often take on too much; they spread their budgets and their energies too thin and become disheartened.

Faced with a new garden, beginners should concentrate on priority areas – areas that will give the greatest return in pleasure for the energy and money expended. This may mean focusing on the front door and ignoring the backyard; it may mean creating a private hideaway and ignoring the neighbours. Every gardener's priorities will be different, but a concentrated effort will always produce the most encouraging results. There will be time enough to expand when one project is successfully completed and the gardener feels able to handle its maintenance.

The Place

Every property comes with a built-in set of givens such as climate, soil and surroundings. Some of the existing characteristics can be modified, others cannot; but the more they are respected, the more successful the garden will be. A gardener may dream of growing rhododendrons in

A concentration of spring plants in a sheltered garden corner overlooked by kitchen or living-room windows provides maximum pleasure for even a modest outlay.

a woodland glade, but if the site is a wind-swept limestone outcrop, realizing the dream will be a losing battle – wind and lime are rhododendrons' chief adversaries.

To get to know a site, draw a plan to scale on squared paper. The plan may not be brilliant, but your pacing around with a tape measure will be a step – or steps – in the right direction. A draftsperson with muddy shoes will at least know something about the lie of the land. Make tracing-paper overlays of different arrangements; it is easier to change ideas on paper than

on the ground. Ideally, the plan will allow for spring plants that complement one another and bloom in sequence.

A succession garden is like a piece of or-chestral music played in slow motion. To keep an interesting composition moving along in harmony, a gardener needs all the skill and experience of a maestro like Ger-trude Jekyll, whose compositions were on the scale of symphonies. Fortunately, she was able to employ a host of gardeners to accompany her.

Symphonies are beyond the reach of

most gardeners, but anyone can keep a simple tune going. One small planting in my garden starts with snowdrops and winter aconites (see illustration). Dwarf irises, glory-of-the-snow and scillas join in, along with a burst of crocuses and then another of species tulips. As the early bulbs fade, pink tulips appear at the back of the bed among the leaves of bearded irises, and at the front, blue grape hyacinths spread through the foliage of cottage pinks. The irises are the climax of the piece. The bright colours of the clove-scented pinks dwindle away with the summer, but their foliage is evergreen and the iris leaves stay handsome for a while. The autumn crocus (*Colchicum*) adds a surprise ending.

An important aspect of place is climate. The map of North America has been divided into climatic zones, which are indicated in diagram form on pages 86 and 87. Lower zone numbers refer to cooler areas; thus zones in Newfoundland range from 3 to 5, while the mildest parts of British Columbia are in zone 9. Canadian and American zones roughly correspond, although Canadian zones are subdivided. The system is handy for quick reference, but it is only a general guide to what will grow where. The factors affecting plant hardiness are complicated, and every garden includes a variety of areas—microclimates—that may vary by several climatic zones.

Somewhere on your land, there may be an ideal spot for an early spring garden, perhaps a south-facing slope backed by the wall of a heated building. I was lucky enough to have just such a place in the angle between the house and the greenhouse. The bulbs I planted there are up and flowering several weeks before their fellows appear among the remnants of winter in the shrubbery, and the pleasure this early garden gives me is out of all proportion to its size. Anyone who doesn't have a ready-made early spot should consider creating one. A well-placed fence or

wall will break the wind and reflect the sun; even a boulder may make a sun trap that will tempt a winter aconite to raise its head in March.

William Wordsworth's famous daffodils grew "beside the lake, beneath the trees," and many other spring flowers, including such wildflowers as trilliums and anemones, look their best scattered under the leafless branches of deciduous trees. However, although the blooms may be over before the trees cast their shade, the plants still need sunlight to build up strength for the following year. If the shade becomes too dense, the plants may fail to flower or may die out altogether. Trees can be thinned to let more sunlight reach the ground. In woodland, this may mean selective felling. Remember that opportunists such as wild raspberries may also take advantage of the extra light—be prepared to step in as referee. In the case of an individual tree, thinning may mean cutting out a few main branches to open up the crown. Phase the work over several years, and never prune more than a third of the branches at any one time.

Not all spring planting benefits from a fast start. If a magnolia is brought along too quickly, the flower buds may be caught by a late frost. It's safer to plant tender flowering shrubs and trees in a slow-warming spot such as an east-facing slope. Baking in the reflected heat of a south-facing foundation wall, a bleeding heart will flower early, but just as quickly, its leaves will yellow and wither. Planted in moist soil and light shade, both the flowers and the foliage will last much longer.

Notice where snowdrifts occur, where trees cast their shade, where structures break the wind and where wide eaves create strips of desert. Such things can mean life or death to a plant. It is obviously impossible to change the geographical situation of a garden, but microclimates can be altered.

When plants winterkill, gardeners tend to blame low temperatures, but often the

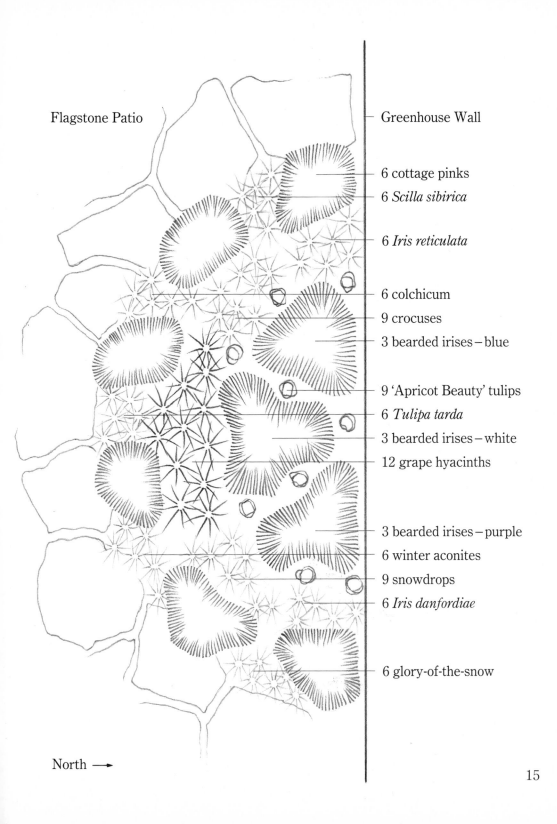

Flagstone Patio

Greenhouse Wall

6 cottage pinks
6 *Scilla sibirica*

6 *Iris reticulata*

6 colchicum
9 crocuses
3 bearded irises – blue

9 'Apricot Beauty' tulips
6 *Tulipa tarda*
3 bearded irises – white
12 grape hyacinths

3 bearded irises – purple
6 winter aconites
9 snowdrops
6 *Iris danfordiae*

6 glory-of-the-snow

North ⟶

real culprits are wind and sun. When the ground freezes, it is difficult for roots to replace the moisture lost by twigs and evergreen leaves and needles. Protecting shrubs and trees from exposure may save them from dehydration. Hedges or slatted fences will break the wind and may give some shade. They can also be used to create snowdrifts – a good snow cover is the ideal protection for many plants that would otherwise be injured or killed by alternate freezing and thawing during the winter. Once the ground is frozen, a snow cover maintains a constant temperature, and plants manage to come through unscathed.

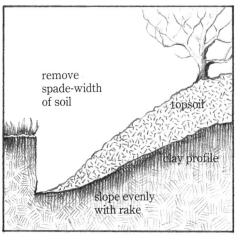

remove spade-width of soil

topsoil

clay profile

slope evenly with rake

A deep shovelled edging on a raised bed is very attractive and easy to maintain.

In areas of clay subsoil, it may be necessary to build raised planting beds (as in the illustration above). To create a simple raised flowerbed in an area of turf, first break up the clay surface of the bed as much as possible; then, using a square-ended spade, cut a trench 6 inches deep around the edge. On the lawn side, the cut must be vertical, while the bed side should be sloped back. Throw the trenched material onto the bed, then mound about nine inches of topsoil on top. Although I don't have a problem with clay in my garden, I still like to build flowerbeds this way.

The trenched edge improves drainage and keeps lawn grasses from wandering into the flowers. More elaborate beds can be raised above ground level using boards, logs, stone or concrete. For shrub planting, the beds should be raised at least 18 inches. Avoid walking on the soil, which compresses it. As most people can reach about two feet for weeding, four feet is a good width for a bed that is accessible from both sides.

Topsoil for a raised bed should drain freely. If a handful of soil squeezed into a lump will not crumble easily, don't use it. The topsoil should also contain plenty of organic material to hold moisture. Add peat moss, rotted manure and compost; in time, they will also help to loosen up the clay base.

Earthy Considerations

There is a sure way to tell the difference between a dabbler and a real gardener. The dabbler thinks that gardeners cultivate plants; the old hand knows that gardeners cultivate the earth. A European writer once explained it this way: if Adam and Eve had been real gardeners, they wouldn't have bothered with the tree of knowledge; they'd have been too busy trying to make off with a barrowload of the heavenly topsoil.

It is easy to imagine what that celestial substance was like. It had the sweet smell of well-decomposed vegetable matter; it was as dark as rich fruitcake and crumbled softly in the hand; it contained exactly the right amounts of all the nutrients and organisms needed for healthy plant growth. In short, it was the perfect compost, the stuff of which every real gardener's dreams are made.

The compost pile is the symbol that finally sets the real gardener apart from the duty gardener and the dabbler. Every soil benefits from additions of such humus. If a garden is built on clay, compost will loosen it up. If it is built on sand, compost

Whatever the scale of a spring garden, good soil and good drainage are priorities.

will help it to hold water. Even the perfect fibrous loam needs compost to keep it that way.

In order to come by that wonderful elixir which turns dirt into gardener's gold, simply take grass clippings or dead leaves and layer them with manure, topsoil, wood ashes and kitchen scraps such as banana skins, apple cores and eggshells. Composting can become a science, but it doesn't have to. Given time, nature will do the trick. Keep the pile damp, and if possible, stir it up now and then—it should decompose in a year or so.

To rot down most efficiently, a compost pile should be several feet deep. To keep it tidy and to keep animals out, it's a good idea to build a bin with sides of slatted wood or chicken wire. The bin should be more or less a cube with sides at least three feet long, and one side should be removable for shovelling. There's a variety of compost bins and barrels available commercially. A pair of bins is ideal— one can serve as the in-bin and the other as the out-bin.

Soil conditions, particularly drainage, are as important as climate in determining a garden layout. When wet earth freezes, the expansion can tear delicate roots apart. I've had plants survive temperatures of minus 13 degrees F in January, only to die from the stress of repeated freezing and thawing in March. In extreme conditions, frost will heave roots right out of the ground. The evergreen crowns of plants like coral bells will rot away if they sit in soggy soil for long. In wet spots, lawn grasses will drown or succumb to fungal diseases.

The moral is clear: don't plant anything in a garden until surface grading and subsoil drainage work properly. All paved and lawn surfaces should slope by at least 1 unit vertically in 60 horizontally. To measure a slope, use a spirit level and a straight board five feet long. Set the level on the board, and rest one end of the board on the highest part of the ground. When the board is horizontal, the other end should be at least one inch above ground level.

For a small fee, provincial departments of agriculture and state extension services will do soil tests. Follow their instructions for collecting soil samples, tell them what kinds of plants are to be grown, and if organic amendments are preferred, let them know. They will check the acidity and nutrient levels in the soil and recommend additions. If, for instance, a property was originally forested with pine, the soil will be acidic and lime should be added before a spring garden is planted.

The Sense of Place

Climate and soil are partly responsible for giving a piece of land a distinct identity; geology and the works of people also come into it. The site may be a bleak hilltop or a crowded city yard, a craggy forest or a flat lot in a subdivision.

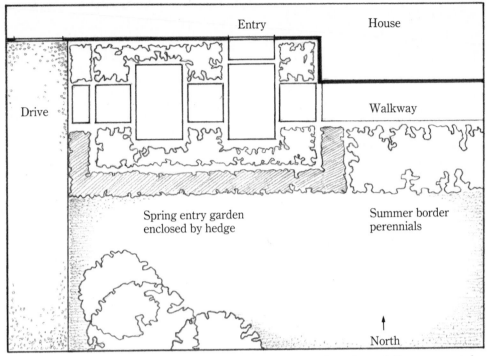

Entry   House

Drive   Walkway

Spring entry garden
enclosed by hedge

Summer border
perennials

North

When a specific area is devoted to spring planting, as in this design, it can revert to *greenery and paving while summer takes over elsewhere in the garden.*

The character of a site is in some respects unalterable, but like climate and soil, it can be modified. The first thing for the gardener to decide is how the garden ought to feel. Cheerful and sunlit? Shady and nostalgic? Impressive? Mysterious? Look at the existing features and decide which will add to that mood and which will detract from it. Make the most of desirable features and be ruthless with the rest. Use only plants and materials that will contribute to the mood. Trilliums and dry stone walling, for instance, will add nothing to a showy formal entrance; concrete pavers and a row of elegant tulips will ruin an atmosphere of woodsy informality.

I am often called onto building sites which have been so thoroughly "landscraped" by heavy equipment that there is little feeling of anything left except desolation. Sometimes I am luckier. At one woodland property, I was consulted long before a backhoe ever reached the

site. We decided upon the position and the level of the house and driveway so that very few trees were disturbed. Mown grass seemed inappropriate, so instead of laying a lawn, we used flagstones to create walkways and patio areas. We pruned the original woodland and added extra shrubs and a few trees, mostly native species. In the entrance court, where the ground was inevitably disturbed, we recreated a small, idealized woodland using shrubs that enjoy a shady situation and mossy boulders saved from the construction site. We also made an effort to salvage woodland soil and were able to establish ferns and native wildflowers such as bunchberries.

In this case, I also had a say in the selection of building materials for the house. We were able to use the same flagstone for both paving and wall finish, so house and garden were "all of a piece" from the start.

More often than not, however, the house already exists, and its character will help determine the garden's. Its layout will also influence the design of a spring garden, which should be readily accessible and, ideally, visible from kitchen or living-room windows. Early spring weather is often unwelcoming and the first flowers modest. If you plant a violet in some distant corner of the garden, who will see it? If you plant it outside the kitchen window, beside the garage door or by the washing line, its progress will be followed as closely as a baby's first tooth.

Like violets, most early-flowering plants are small. The northern landscape, by contrast, is often large and open. A handful of crocuses planted in an acre of lawn will look like stray candy wrappers. There are two alternatives: plant a thousand crocuses, or plant a few crocuses in an intimate setting. My accidental spring garden is simply part of the larger garden, but it is defined by the shade of the linden tree.

When the scale of the landscape threatens to overwhelm the scale of the planting, consider creating a garden within a garden (see illustration on facing page). Enclose a space (using a hedge, a fence, a wall or even a change of level), and create a small-scale garden inside it. Such a spot provides the owner with some privacy and can give the visitor a pleasant surprise. Consider using only flowering plants and paving materials in this area, keeping lawn for the wider world. The concentration of detail and colour can create a big impact; it's like keeping your treasures in an open jewel box.

One of the most famous gardens of this type is at Sissinghurst Castle in England. The property was designed as a series of compartments, and one of these — the Lime Walk — is devoted to spring plantings. The arrangement is formal: a flagstone path runs between wide beds brimming with spring flowers such as anemones, fritillarias, narcissi and grape hyacinths; trained lime (linden) trees bor-

Small flowers such as Anemone blanda *are attractive in naturalized profusion.*

der the walk, and the whole is enclosed by a rectangle of high hedges. Most of the year, the beds lie quiet. The garden, however, is still attractive. So strong is the structure of walls, trees and paving that one scarcely notices the absence of bloom.

Occasionally, a garden is given over entirely to spring planting, which makes sense if the owner spends most of the summer at the cottage. It also makes sense to those who find the range of spring flowers so appealing that they'll willingly trade nine months of mediocrity for three months of undiluted pleasure. If such gardeners take their cue from Sissinghurst and build a strong framework into their garden design, the nine months will be more acceptable, and the three, more delightful. In other words, it is fine to put all your eggs in one basket — as long as you have a basket.

Plan of Action

In fall, garden centres mount glamorous displays of coloured posters showing flowering bulbs in all their spring glory. The temptation is too much; impulsive gardeners arrive home laden with fancy tulips and assorted daffodils on special offer. But where to put them? While gar- 19 deners ponder the problem, the bags of bulbs go into the garage, and sad to relate, that's where many of them stay. I've often been asked if it's worth planting dried-up bulbs left over from a buying spree the year before. It isn't.

Even if one manages to plant the bulbs while they are fresh, things may not turn out the way one hoped. Bulbs set hastily in unsuitable soil may manage to squeeze out a flower the following spring, but as the years go by, they are sure to be a disappointment. Long-term success with bulbs requires some forethought. In fall, there is no foliage to indicate which bulbs have been planted where; it is sickening to slice into the flesh of a hidden tulip and disconcerting to find a crop of old daffodils springing up through a planting of new fritillarias. It is also discouraging to wreck a planting in order to make room for a drainpipe or a new tree.

The work of constructing, planting and maintaining a spring garden follows a logical sequence. It is a waste of money to buy plants before preparing the soil and a waste of time to prepare the soil before attending to the drainage. A little planning saves a lot of backache – and a lot of heartache too.

The planning comes in two stages. First, the design: whether it's on paper or in your head, be sure you have a clear idea of your goal. Once you know where you're going, you can start working out how to get there. The plan of action is the second stage; it's a matter of getting jobs done in the right order – which isn't always easy. The following checklist may be useful in plotting a course through a minefield of garden bloopers.

Spring 1

Grading and Drainage

Don't proceed until the answer to each of the following questions is yes.

• Does surface water run freely off all parts of the property?
• Does surface water run away from buildings?
• Is the outflow from footing drains running unobstructed?
• Is roof water led off harmlessly?
• Does the driveway have a good base? Does it drain quickly without washing out?

Construction

• Complete all driveways, walls, walks, patios and other work involving hard materials and heavy equipment.

Pruning

• Remove all dead trees and limbs; thin out trees or branches where more light is required.

Topsoil

• Bring in topsoil where necessary.
• Have existing and new soil tested. Amend as advised.
• Cultivate planting areas to an appropriate depth.
• Start a compost pile.

Planting

• Plant new trees and shrubs, keeping in mind their mature size, the position of overhead wires and underground cables, as well as the activities of children, dogs and snowploughs.
• Plant perennials. Beware of invasive plants, either purchased or donated. Be sure to mark the positions of plants such as Virginia bluebells, which have ephemeral foliage.

Summer 1

Maintenance

• Water generously.
• Weed well. A weed in time saves 90.

- Dead-head perennials and young rhododendrons.

Propagation

- Start perennials from seeds or cuttings as described in Chapter Three.

Fall 1

Planting

- Plant trees and shrubs.
- Plant bulbs. Daffodils should go in early; tulips can be planted until freeze-up. Be sure to keep a record of their positions and names.

Winterizing

- Take the time to clean up unsightly and bulky remains of perennials, while leaving attractive stems and light foliage in place.
- Spray tender evergreens with anti-desiccant.
- Protect newly planted evergreens from the effects of wind and sun; use burlap screens (which tend to be ugly but effective) or snow fencing.
- After freeze-up, lay boughs of spruce and fir over perennials to keep the ground frozen until spring.

Spring 2

Spring Cleaning

- Remove brushwood cover at the first sign of bulbs.
- Tidy up winter debris *carefully*. Emerging sprouts should be handled delicately, as they are easily damaged.

Planting

- Plant trees and shrubs.
- Plant, transplant and divide perennials.

Beautiful, vigorous blooms reward careful bed preparation and maintenance.

- Transplant snowdrops and winter aconites while the foliage is still green.
- Make a note of positions and types of bulbs to be added in fall.

Maintenance

- Feed bulbs with fertilizer high in nitrogen.
- Dead-head bulbs unless the seed is to be saved or self-sown.
- Allow bulb foliage to mature, then remove and compost.

Finally, stand and stare. Remember, the lovely colours, scents and sounds of the spring garden are what make it all worthwhile.

Elspeth Bradbury, a landscape architect in private practice in New Brunswick, is also a keen gardener and enjoys writing and broadcasting on landscaping and garden topics.

Chapter Two:
Spring Flower Bulbs

By Helen Chesnut

For a devoted gardener – as for a compulsive theatregoer – much pleasure lies in anticipation. And for the gardener, no time brings keener anticipation than spring. My garden of nine years is now sufficiently established that I know all the players by name and cheer each one on stage at the appointed time. But it wasn't always so. When my family moved to this property on a half acre of partly cleared forest in British Columbia, we faced a mammoth rock-removal job – by bulldozers and by hand – and it was hard to look beyond the boulders to a time when the first bulbs could be planted. Now, the remaining immovable boulders have become the setting for some of the earliest scenes of the spring drama: a carpet of 'Yellow Mammoth' crocuses, a clump of deep violet *Iris reticulata*, a cluster of nodding snowdrops and buttercup-yellow winter aconites. And these are but a hint of the pageant already gathering its forces elsewhere in the garden. ᐧᐧᐧ Patches of snow crocuses spread their sheets of colour in warm and sunny sites, and the tiny orchidlike Danford iris is ready for close-up viewing beside garden pathways. The large-flowered Dutch crocus appears with *Iris reticulata* and the first of the species (wild) tulips and daffodils. Here in my garden, Lent lily (*Narcissus lobularis*), a miniature trumpet daffodil, blooms with species tulips around the beginning of Lent each 23 year. Then the delightful daisy-flowered *Anemone blanda* will burst into flower in white, pink and blue, and the water-lily tulips (*Tulipa kaufmanniana*) will open wide their blossoms to the sun.

The daffodil season continues with more miniatures and the cheering hosts of trumpet daffodils, which herald their large-cupped cousins along with the startling blue Siberian squills and the Greigii tulips with their richly striped foliage. At this point, the hyacinths step in, perfuming house and garden with the high-scented breath of spring, and grape hyacinths cover their grassy foliage with sheets of blue.

Double daffodils and heavily fragrant jonquils wind up the daffodil season, as crown imperials (*Fritillaria imperialis*) produce imposing clusters of golden, orange or red bells, and single and double early tulips begin flowering. Sturdy, large-flowered Triumphs and Darwin Hybrids lead the garden into a midseason of tulip bloom, with a glorious procession of late tulips to follow in a lively diversity of flower styles. This last May-June phase of the spring bulb drama will also see ornamental onions (*Allium* spp), Spanish bluebells (*Scilla campanulata*) and white starry-flowered mounds of star of Bethlehem (*Ornithogalum umbellatum*).

Planning and Planting

Where in the garden to arrange selected plantings from all this spring-flowering splendour is largely a matter of personal taste and common sense, provided the gardener keeps in mind any special needs of a particular bulb. You can't go too far wrong by planting the more delicate miniature types, such as the small species daffodils and tulips, in little spots of their own – at the front of flowerbeds, beside pathways, in odd corners where they can be appreciated at close range and not be overrun by exuberant nearby plantings. The more robust low-growing spring bulbs like large Dutch crocuses and water-lily tulips serve well as edgings and as neat flowering collars under trees, fitting also into limited spaces around and between shrubs and perennials. The taller spring bulbs add dramatic splashes of colour grouped in similar, bigger spaces or in display beds of their own. Daffodils are especially well suited to surrounding with ground covers such as aubrieta or arabis. Spring bulb flowers lend themselves best to casual groupings. Avoid planting them in rows or in stiffly formal patterns. Loose ovals or roughly triangular arrangements with a few bulbs drifting a little away from the corners and ends will give a pleasantly natural effect.

Most of the small bulbs can be established in their appointed sites over the long term – a practice called naturalizing or perennializing. The difference between the terms lies in the nature of the planting site: one might naturalize bulbs in a woodland or grassy setting and perennialize them among foundation plantings or in perennial and shrub beds. Whatever the site or the term used, keep in mind these points:
• The foliage will need sun in order to mature properly after flowering.
• Grass cutting will have to wait till the foliage-ripening process is complete to ensure flowering the following spring.

In all cases, select sites in full or nearly full sun, but take some care in shading daffodils with orange crowns (the flower centres): a little shelter from hot sun will preserve their rich colouring for the longest possible time. In perennial and shrub beds, allow bulbs enough room to avoid disturbing the roots of neighbouring plants. Avoid sites around trees with shallow root systems that would present too much competition. All bulbs need a well-drained soil – none will flourish in soggy conditions. Before planting, dig the site over as deeply as possible and mix in some peat moss, compost or old manure along with a handful of bone meal scattered over

Ideal candidates for naturalizing, daffodils and scillas enhance each other in mixed plantings, in clumps throughout a border or on the edge of a wooded area.

each square yard. At planting time, the soil should be just moderately moist.

To plant each bulb, first dig a hole large enough to allow the base of the bulb to rest at the depth suggested for its type in the bulb list at the end of this chapter. A trowel with depth marks inscribed on the blade and a tubular bulb planter are handy aids for making the holes quickly. Settle each bulb in its hole, firm the soil over it and mark its place. Use a little dusting of lime if the soil is acidic, a dollop of peat moss if it is alkaline. Marking the site of each bulb allows one to keep track of plantings and helps in spacing the bulbs accurately and evenly.

For special bulbs and in special display beds (if one has the space and wishes to try this form of bulb-growing), take out a deeper hole than is needed, and mix well into the bottom a teaspoon of bone meal and a small handful of peat moss or compost. Brush a little soil over this, and set in the bulb – the new roots will appreciate something extra to bite into.

As a general rule, in fall plant the earliest-flowering bulbs first – snowdrops and crocuses, for example, and the species tulips and daffodils. All daffodils benefit from as early a planting as possible, as they are naturally early rooters. Keep the soil in areas planted with bulbs evenly moistened during the autumn, and in cold areas, begin to mulch after the first few hard frosts – straw or hay, sawdust, wood shavings, chopped dry leaves and pine needles are all suitable. Add more layers as the weather grows colder. Pray for a nice snow cover too, or pile on snow from round about, and over it lay a few light branches or evergreen boughs to hold it all together. As winter draws to a close, the procedure is reversed. It is crucial to remove layers of mulch early enough that it is all gone when the shoots nose through the soil, or they will grow peculiarly twisted or be damaged as the mulch is removed. Be particularly careful with the last layer. Set the mulch beside the planting so that you can re-cover the bed in case of an untimely return of winter cold.

Bulb Care

As the first tips of growth start to nudge through the soil in spring, lightly cultivate around them, removing any weeds and mixing a very light scattering of compost 25 into the top layer of soil. Then give yourself over to the sheer enjoyment of watching for fat flower buds and anticipating the many delights of bulb flowers that bloom in the spring.

Post-bloom care will ensure another good show of flowers the following spring:
• Dead-head flowers as they fade, leaving the stem to help replenish the bulb.
• Pick up fallen tulip petals as a disease-prevention measure.
• Mark definitely chosen sites for planting more bulbs in fall (use a conspicuous label, and write a reminder to purchase on the calendar).
• Use stakes of different heights as a key for other prospective plantings and an aid to decision making.

Sun, air circulation and clean ground contribute to long-term health of bulbs.

• Lift withered foliage when it pulls out of the ground easily, and clean away any surface debris.
• As a reminder, use a thin layer of peat moss, vermiculite or even perlite to mark the site of dormant bulbs.

If you have tried a display bed of midseason and late tulips and wish to replace them with summer bedding plants, you may lift and transplant the bulbs immediately after flowering, digging each one carefully (keeping soil around the bulb)

and transplanting it straightaway into a site with good soil in the vegetable garden or some out-of-the-way spot. There, with a watering-in using a transplanting solution, the plants will continue to ripen, and the bulbs can be harvested for replanting as usual.

Spring bulb flowers are notably free of most of the miseries to which other kinds of plants are prone. But keep in mind a few wise cultural practices to help prevent rotting and diseases:
• Plant only clean bulbs with no dark splotches or signs of mould.
• Choose open, sunny sites with freely circulating air and well-drained soil.
• Keep the ground in and around bulb plantings cleared of weeds and debris.
• As the plants grow, dig out any suspicious-looking ones. This "roguing" eliminates sources of contamination; destroy both plants and bulbs – do not compost.

In rainy, humid weather, tulips may be afflicted by botrytis, or "fire," which produces grey mould spots on leaves and flowers. Dig infected plants along with a two-inch layer of surrounding soil, and put them in a bag for immediate disposal; otherwise, disease spores will spread.

The narcissus bulb fly – greater (like a bumblebee) and lesser (like a small wasp) – lays eggs at the base of a bulb, usually a daffodil, where the maggots then feed, rotting the bulbs. Early in spring, before the grubs can leave the bulbs and hatch into adult flies, dig any bulbs with suspiciously skinny growth and no flowers. Hilling up the soil over daffodils when the spent foliage is removed can help act as a deterrent, and ground covers make access to the plant bases more difficult for the flies.

Rodents chomping on bulbs can be discouraged by a resident cat, by planting within the confines of wire cages or by planting close to the house. Daffodil bulbs and foliage are immune – they are toxic, and rodents know it. Some gardeners report good success in repelling all manner

Less hardy bulbs such as Fritillaria melea-gris *may succeed in special sites.*

of beasts with plantings of the skunk-scented crown imperials.

A problem in cold-winter gardens may be frost damage. There, the hardiest bulbs available will form the backbone of the spring display. The greatest range of plant size, flower type and colour will come with the tulips, which will also provide a long season of bloom if cultivars of early, midseason and late types are chosen. Siberian squills (*Scilla sibirica*) and grape hyacinths (*Muscari*) are useful and hardy, as are the less well-known pusch-kinia and camassia.

It is possible to push beyond climatic limits by planting not-quite-hardy bulbs in very carefully selected sites, such as against a warm and sheltered house wall or in a protected courtyard corner. Try marginally hardy spring bulbs such as cro-cuses and daffodils, snowdrops (*Galan-thus*), glory-of-the-snow (*Chionodoxa*), fritillarias and flowering onions (*Allium*).

Potted Bulbs

The final answer to growing spring bulbs too cold-tender for the winter cli-mate is to plant them in pots, winter them in a protected place and bring them out to bloom in the spring. This is quite like growing bulbs in pots for winter or early spring indoor bloom, commonly called forcing, except that the bulbs are planted more in the fashion of those grown out-doors—more deeply and in deeper pots.

I use mostly six- and eight-inch-wide nursery pots that are at least as deep as they are wide. I fill the pots barely half full with a gently firmed-down soil mix before settling the bases of such large bulbs as hyacinths and daffodils on the soil surface close together but not touching. Then I sift more soil mix in between and over the bulbs and carefully firm it. Smaller bulbs are settled on a layer of soil mix that fills the pots by about two-thirds. The planted pots are watered and allowed to drain well.

It pays to be very careful in selecting bulbs for potting. Avoid especially any with mould, and use a fast-draining, sterile planting mixture purchased ready-made or blended at home. My own preferred blend is roughly one-third each of steri-lized potting soil, damp peat moss and per-lite. To each two-gallon pailful, I add about two tablespoons of bone meal.

Where these potted surprise packages are to be sheltered will depend upon the severity of a typical winter. Bulbs that are almost hardy for your climatic zone will probably receive enough protection at the bottom of a trench dug near a house wall with some insulating material such as sawdust, wood chips, perlite or shredded Styrofoam surrounding the pots and covering their tops to a depth of about 27

Excellent for indoor potting, hyacinths are also beautiful in massed outdoor plantings.

Grown this way, they can also be used as cut flowers.

eight inches. Other good places would be inside cold attics, cellars and unheated basement rooms or against a garage wall that adjoins the house. In interior locations, watch that the soil does not dry during the winter, and cover the pots loosely with newspaper or with inverted pots with drainage holes.

Ideally, potted bulbs should start their rooting period at around 50 degrees F and chill to around freezing until the weather begins to warm in spring. Toward the end of winter, begin more regular checks of the bulbs and gradually uncover them. In spring, when top shoots begin to sprout, bring the pots out and dig them into the garden where you want to display the flowers. Cover the pot rims with soil, and astound your neighbours and friends.

Bulb forcing is a similar process. Nothing cheers a long winter like a potful of brightly blooming spring bulbs that have been gently persuaded to flower before their usual time. In this procedure, which is geared strictly for indoor bloom, I select the plumpest, heaviest bulbs in the most perfect condition I can find and plant them in the same sterile, fast-draining planting mix described for outdoor pots. For a really full bouquet, I pack as many bulbs as possible into the pot without allowing the bulbs to touch each other or the pot sides. For large bulbs, I use regular pots and leave the tips just barely exposed above the soil line. I use shallow pots for the small bulbs and cover their tips with one inch of the soil mix. Watered thoroughly, the pots are ready to set in a cold, dark place to form roots.

An ideal temperature range for the rooting period is 41 to 48 degrees F. Wherever there is natural light, cover the planted pots with clean inverted pots, thick paper cones or cardboard boxes. Prop the boxes up a little, and ventilate the cones by leaving a hole at the top so that air can circulate while darkness is maintained.

Most tulips, daffodils and hyacinths need 10 to 12 weeks to form roots. Others require only about 8 weeks, including the especially fast and easy daffodils 'Cragford' and 'February Gold,' prepared hyacinth bulbs that have already been given some cold treatment, and some of the small bulbs—snow and Dutch crocuses, dwarf irises and grape hyacinths, for example. During this period, do not let the soil dry, and check on root development as the weeks go by. As soon as roots appear at the drainage holes and top growth is between one and two inches tall, bring the pots into a cool, semidark spot in the living area of the house. After a week, they can be placed in bright light to bloom. Coolish room temperatures combined with bright light yield the sturdiest plants and the most vividly coloured, long-lasting flowers possible.

I calculate three to four weeks between rooting and bloom. Adding this to the estimated rooting time allows me to aim at flowers for special occasions such as Christmas or Valentine's Day. For example, a shallow, five-inch-wide pot planted in late September with three prepared hyacinth bulbs will have produced roots and short shoots by the end of November. Brought gradually into warmth and light, the bulbs should be in bloom by the third or fourth week of December. It is possible to delay bloom simply by holding rooted pots in cold storage until you are ready to start the flowering process. Bulbs can also be potted in succession for a steady supply of spring flowers indoors.

For bloom all at once, use only one cultivar per pot. Several pots in bloom can be gathered together in a basket or other large container for a combination spring garden indoors.

Another way to have spring flowers indoors is, of course, to cut them. My favourites for cut-flower bouquets are tulips and daffodils, but many of the small bulbs make charming arrangements too. The best spring bulbs for cut flowers are indicated in the following bulb list. Leave as much foliage as possible intact when gathering cut flowers; it keeps the plants working and the bulbs revitalized after bloom. Cut tulips with either just the bare stem or one green leaf only to preserve the bulb. A long diagonal cut and the use of a floral preservative will facilitate the intake of water. Tulips in all but the tallest vases take on lovely natural curves as the stems arch and bend gracefully under the weight of the blooms—an enchanting sight one notices everywhere in Holland at tulip time.

Cut daffodil stems exude a sap that can cause tulips and some other flowers to wilt. Either arrange daffodils in a container of their own, or keep them in a separate one for about 16 hours before rinsing the stems and mixing them with other flowers. Charcoal at the rate of one tablespoon per quart of water or a few drops of bleach will help to deactivate any lingering sap. All cut-flower arrangements respond to a cool site out of direct sun and a cool place overnight.

On the following pages, selected spring bulbs are listed alphabetically with 29 specific information on hardiness, height, time of bloom, soil needs, planting depths and more. All of these will vary, of course, with the conditions in any particular garden and, for that matter, in any particular spring. Although the term "bulb" is commonly used as a kind of umbrella to cover a variety of structures that provide nourishment for the emerging flower and anchor the plant in the ground, it is part of their fascination and mystery that only some are true bulbs; others are formed in different ways and are classified as corms, tubers, tuberous roots or rhizomes. At planting time, there is already, at the centre of the true bulb only, a miniature embryonic flower that could be seen and recognized if the bulb were cut open.

When selecting bulbs locally from display bins, look for clean surfaces with no signs of mould. Check particularly the tip and base of the bulb, which should be clean and undamaged. Bulbs should be firm, and the larger kinds should feel solid and heavy in the hand.

Chosen, planted and tended with care, the flowers will become old friends, dreamed of in the gloomiest days of winter and welcomed with the delight of recognition each year as winter leaves the stage to spring.

Allium spp

(flowering onion, ornamental onion)

Allium aflatunense 'Purple Sensation' (May to June) forms beautiful, densely packed, rounded heads of purple-lilac flowers on 3-foot stems. Plant bulbs 10 inches apart and 8 inches deep. *A. giganteum* (June to July), at 67 inches, is the goliath among the flowering onions, with huge spheres of shining lilac flowers. Plant 12 inches apart and 8 inches deep. *A. karataviense* (May to June) bears on 9-inch stems round heads of white flowers that are delicately shaded in silvery rose tones. The foliage is broad and decorative. This allium is said to be wonderful for

growing in pots—a project I have yet to try. Plant 8 inches apart and 6 inches deep. *A. sphaerocephalum* (June to July), sometimes called drumsticks, produces cone-shaped flower heads of bright crimson-maroon on 2-foot stems. Plant 4 inches apart and 4 inches deep.

Allium moly, *A. oreophilum* and *A. neapolitanum* are a terrific trio of low-growing ornamental onions, blooming in the same May-to-June period on stems 10 inches tall. They are easy to fit into many sites—in the rock garden, in groupings adjacent to perennials such as coral bells and around spring-flowering deciduous shrubs and trees. *A. moly*, golden garlic, has attractive, broadly straplike grey-green foliage and bright yellow flowers in loose clusters. Plant 3 inches apart and 4 inches deep. *A. oreophilum* (sometimes sold as *A. ostrowskianum*) bears small heads of pink flowers and straplike leaves. Plant 4 inches apart and 4 inches deep. *A. neapolitanum* produces very graceful, loose clusters of dainty white flowers. This is the tenderest of the low-growing alliums and needs winter protection in colder zones. Plant 6 inches apart and 4 inches deep. All the alliums make outstanding cut flowers. The low-growing ones are good for pots and for naturalizing, while the tall kinds are useful for attractive accents in perennial and shrub beds. The big alliums benefit from an extra mulch covering in cold-winter areas. Most alliums dry well and make delightful additions to everlasting bouquets.

Anemone spp

(windflower)

Anemone blanda, Greek anemone or Grecian windflower, grows from a tuber and forms ferny mounds of finely divided foliage and bright daisylike flowers in white, pink, blue and mixed colours. Its flowers are long-lasting, and where hardy, it is a most versatile spring flower, useful for edging beds, for planting in drifts around shrubs and trees and for separating plantings of taller spring bulbs such as early tulips and daffodils. A cultivar such as 'White Splendour' makes a stunning path-edge display beneath red tulips or mixed with grape hyacinths. Sometimes of dubious hardiness even where it is theoretically hardy, *A. blanda* planted in areas colder than zone 6 will benefit from a deep winter mulch cover or a siting that offers some protection. Where it is hardy, *A. blanda* perennializes well. Plant tubers 3 inches apart and 3 inches deep.

The European wood anemone (*Anemone nemorosa*) is one of my favourite spring flowers. Its delicate, star-shaped, pale lilac flowers rise gracefully on 6-inch stems above a solid patch of fresh, green, ferny foliage in an open area between rhododendrons in my garden. Though said to be invasive, I have not yet found it so. The wood anemone naturalizes easily for use in open woodland situations or between shrubs, and it combines beautifully with

miniature daffodils, protecting their lower portions against the narcissus bulb fly, a real problem in my gardening area. I find my plantings just about care-free, though they do welcome a thin layer of compost or old manure over their site before top growth begins.

Camassia cusickii

This North American wildflower blooms at tulip time, its spikes of large, blue, star-shaped flowers with golden anthers set off by long, straplike leaves. Camassia makes a fine cut flower and in the garden is effective massed together and set against a sunny fenceline or naturalized in grass. In a rich, moist soil, camassia will perennialize with little care on the West Coast and in other mild places, though a small amount of old manure or compost around the plants just prior to bloom is helpful in 31

ciduous trees and shrubs. Because the foliage dies down quickly after flowering has finished, plantings are well suited to the front of a perennial flowerbed or the rock garden. Chionodoxa associates well with low ground covers such as rock cress (arabis). Though the stems are short, the cut flowers last well. Chionodoxa produces a full and lovely display in pots, as each stem carries about eight flowers. In the garden, plant bulbs 3 inches apart and 4 inches deep.

keeping the soil enriched. Plant 8 inches apart and 5 inches deep. Plants grow about 3 feet tall.

Chionodoxa spp

(glory-of-the-snow)

I first made the acquaintance of this versatile and sprightly spring bulb in a bag of small bulbs my father sent me from his garden late one summer years ago. I planted them in the grass around a dwarf sour cherry tree. The following spring, as the tree came alive in a cloud of white bloom, the ground below responded with profuse bouquets of upward-facing, white-centred, bright sky-blue flowers. That was *Chionodoxa luciliae*, the most popular and commonly grown species (4 to 5 inches in height). *C.l.* 'Rosea' is a light pink form, and *C.l.* 'Gigantea' is taller and larger-flowered with light blue flowers.

Glory-of-the-snow is prized for its earliness, easy-growing nature and adaptability. The bulbs naturalize easily and are lovely planted in casual drifts beneath de-

Convallaria majalis

(lily-of-the-valley)

Lily-of-the-valley is a big May event in my house and garden. From the carpets of fresh, broad, apple-green foliage and sturdy sprays of spotless white flowers, I gather bouquets for the kitchen table, where the elegantly scalloped bells and their strong, sweet scent can be fully savoured at close quarters. Sometimes, I mix in the slender spikes of coral bells, a perennial flower that begins blooming at the same time. Lily-of-the-valley flower

multiply rapidly into clumps of grassy foliage with many blooms, they are excellent for naturalizing just about anywhere in the garden where a flowering signal of winter's passing would be welcome – under deciduous trees and shrubs, between perennials, at the edges of flowerbeds, in rock gardens – and they give a most effective display when planted in splashes of one colour.

stems also dry surprisingly well for pretty everlasting bouquets.

Convallaria prefers a partially shaded site in a moist, humus-rich soil. Plant the pips in autumn or early spring, setting them 4 inches apart and 1 inch deep. Thereafter, maintain the humus content of the soil by covering the planting with a layer of compost or old manure in early spring. Valuable as a low-maintenance ground cover, the plants naturalize so easily that they can become invasive. To avoid this problem, sink barriers around the planting or dig straying rhizomes yearly. Lift and thin the planting when it becomes overcrowded.

Crocus spp

Large Dutch crocuses, harbingers of spring in many home gardens, greet the first hints of warmth by unfolding shining faces to the sun. Because crocus corms

Large Dutch crocuses can be naturalized in grass wherever the lawn does not require cutting too early; to ripen properly, the foliage needs to grow freely for several weeks following bloom. I can clearly recall the delight on the faces of our two young children one spring when they noticed the crocus "happy faces" their father had arranged in the lawn outside our living-room window. Crocus corms set close together in a shallow pot and covered with an inch of soil produce a wonderful display of colour in the house. Outdoors in the garden, plant them 2 inches apart for a full display quickly or 4 inches apart if they are to be left several years for 33 naturalizing; in either case, set the corms 4 inches deep.

Species, or snow, crocuses bloom one or two weeks earlier than Dutch crocuses and are a little less hardy and a bit smaller in bloom and stature. They come in a splendid variety of colours and offer many an adventure to the home gardener, whether as a potted delight or in any of the first-to-warm spots in the garden. Look for particularly stunning colours among cultivars of *Crocus chrysanthus*. Crocuses do not require a rich soil, but they do need very good drainage. And although light shade, as under high-limbed deciduous trees, is fine for the post-bloom period, the flowers will give their best open-faced showing in full sun. A warm and sheltered sunny site will give the earliest bloom; but for a prolonged period of crocus bloom, plant some of the same cultivars in less protected areas as well.

Eranthis hyemalis

(winter aconite)

Winter aconites come into bloom with snowdrops at the start of the spring bulb season, bringing to the garden patches of shining golden buttercup bloom, each 4-inch-tall flower set off by a perky ruff of green foliage at its base. Home gardeners who enjoy, as I do, the lighthearted combination of yellow and white will be pleased with adjacent plantings of these two extra-early flowers. Use eranthis anywhere early gold would serve well to brighten the garden: along a pathway edge, between paving blocks, in woodland areas, in rock gardens. As the tubers benefit from a little cooling shade in summer, sites beneath and between deciduous trees and shrubs are ideal. In congenial situations, winter aconites will naturalize well. They are good for growing in raised areas for close appreciation of the interesting blooms. A warm, sheltered site will yield the earliest flowers.

Plant the tubers as early as possible in a moist but well-drained, humus-rich soil. If the tubers seem dry, plump them in moist peat moss prior to planting. After they have become established, if you wish to move some plants, don't wait until the foliage dies back as with most spring bulbs; move them, keeping the soil around the roots, while the plants are still green. Plant 3 inches apart and 4 inches deep. Winter aconites are also suitable for pot culture.

Erythronium spp

(trout lily, dog's-tooth violet)

April is enlivened in our garden by a view through patio doors of two large clumps of erythronium – 'White Beauty' and 'Yellow Pagoda.' The yellow-flowered planting in partial shade is taller (18 inches) and looser in habit than the white, which has attractively mottled leaves and grows to 12 inches. Both are well-established plantings bearing many gracefully nodding lilylike blooms with reflexed (backward-bending) petals.

the robust stem, a large cluster of hanging bells unfolds, topped by a lively tuft of green leaves. Given a moist but well-drained, humus-rich soil, they are most satisfying plants to grow and appear in yellow, brick-red and orange forms. The bulbs and flowers both have a strong musky odour reminiscent of skunk—a scent that many home gardeners find useful in deterring moles and other rodents from feasting on nearby bulb plantings. In groups of three or five, crown imperials add colourful and interesting accents to perennial and shrub beds. I find small groupings ideal for setting between peonies. As the fritillaria foliage fades after flowering, it is quickly camouflaged by the rising peony stems.

The large bulbs will perennialize satisfactorily if they are grown in sun with plentiful water and a cooling mulch layer or ground cover over them during the summer. Like the lilies to which they are related, they must never be allowed to dry. Plant *Fritillaria imperialis* 6 inches

Erythroniums thrive in light shade or dappled sun in a moist, peaty, woodsy soil; they will not survive in heat or dry conditions. It is helpful to mulch plantings with peat moss and compost in August. Erythroniums are ideal for long-term naturalizing in woodland settings or locating in the cool shade of shrubs and trees. They associate well with primroses and violets. As well, they can be lifted carefully as they begin poking through the ground and fitted into a pot where their blooms can be enjoyed in a cool spot indoors. Plant the bulbs 4 inches apart and 3 inches deep.

Fritillaria spp

(fritillary)

The most imposing plants among the fritillarias are the crown imperials (*Fritillaria imperialis*), which shoot through the ground with great vigour, the flower stems quickly lengthening to a yard or more above glossy foliage. At the top of

35

deep and 10 to 12 inches apart in a deeply dug, fast-draining soil to which materials such as peat moss, compost or old manure have been added to help ensure a cool, moist root run. Plant as early as possible, while the bulbs are fresh and plump.

At the other end of the fritillaria height scale is *Fritillaria meleagris*, commonly called the snake's head fritillary, guinea hen flower or checkered lily. These plants also produce delightful, nodding, bell-like flowers but only one or two on each wiry 10-inch stem. The blooms are unique for their checkered purple-and-white pattern, although there is a white cultivar as well. *F. meleagris* gives a charming display in situations similar to its native haunts under trees and in meadows. In the garden, groupings beneath trees and shrubs or in grassy areas will be pleasantly showy, as will plantings among perennial flowers, in the rock garden and in pots. Plant 4 inches apart and 4 inches deep.

A personal favourite is *Fritillaria persica*, which produces sweet-scented, deep plum-purple bells along the upper portion of its 32-inch flower stem. It is grown and used in the same way as crown imperials.

Galanthus spp

(snowdrop)

Familiar and cherished for their sprightly white bells drooping from wiry 4- to 6-inch stems, snowdrops associate pleasantly with the shiny buttercup-yellow of winter aconite (*Eranthis*), which blooms at the same time. The common snowdrop (*Galanthus nivalis*) also comes in a double-flowered form. *G. elwesii* has large flowers on slightly taller stems. Plant snowdrops in any situation where the very early white flowers can be fully appreciated: in rock gardens, beneath trees and shrubs, naturalized in wooded areas or in low ground covers such as creeping thyme, phlox or arabis (rock cress), which protect the flowers from splashing dirt. Sites beneath deciduous trees and shrubs will allow the

foliage to mature properly in the sun before the plants above them leaf out. The foliage ripens fast, making snowdrops ideally suited to sites at the front of garden beds.

Snowdrops will naturalize indefinitely in moist soil with ample humus. Plant the bulbs 3 inches apart and 4 inches deep. As with winter aconite, move snowdrops after flowering and while the foliage is still green. If growing them in pots, keep the plants as cool as possible when they are brought into the house to flower.

Hyacinthus spp

(hyacinth)

Though snowdrops and crocuses are the most familiar flowering heralds of the new season, it is the hyacinth that brings the sweet, fragrant breath of spring to house and garden. The easiest of all spring bulbs to grow in pots in the house, the hyacinth produces large, dense spikes of waxy, bell-shaped flowers in white, pink, blue, yellow, red, salmon or orange. The size of the flower spike is directly related to the size of the bulb, the largest bulbs producing spikes that are almost too large, heavy and breakable for outdoor planting.

Like most spring bulbs, hyacinths look best planted in groups of one colour, alone or adjacent to groupings of another, compatible colour. To avoid a stiffly formal look, plant in rounded or oval groups of uneven numbers rather than in rows. Arrange such plantings under deciduous shrubs, toward the front of flower borders, along pathways and by doorways to take full advantage of the appealing scent.

Hyacinth bulbs have a tendency to split, producing in their second year flower spikes that are looser, less formal and pleasantly graceful. However, when they become too thin, dig the bulbs and replant only the largest. I've had a planting of hyacinths remain in fat-spiked flowering form between some hydrangea bushes for five years now, probably because the site is perfectly drained and I top the soil yearly with peat moss and compost.

Using top-sized hyacinth bulbs the first autumn for potting is an excellent way to enjoy these exquisite flowers close by at their most plump and lavish. These same bulbs, allowed to ripen in the pot after flowering, may be planted outdoors early in the fall and will produce less opulent, more weather-resistant flower spikes the following spring.

Pot three bulbs to a 5-inch-wide pot, or five to a 6-inch pot. Barely cover the bulb tips with planting mix. Pretreated hyacinth bulbs have already been given some of their cold treatment and can almost certainly be counted on for Christmas blossoming. Outdoors in zones 4 to 6, give hyacinth bulbs a sheltered spot, avoiding wet sites, and mulch for the winter with some loose material such as wood chips. Plant 6 inches apart and 8 inches deep.

Iris spp

(iris)

The Danford iris (*Iris danfordiae*) – earliest of the miniatures – often flowers as early as January in my British Columbia garden, about two weeks after the snowdrops begin to bloom. This dwarf (5-inch) iris bears bright little lemon-yellow flowers with attractive dark freckling. Plant the bulbs where the intricate blooms can be appreciated at close hand: at the front of a flowerbed, tucked into up-front corners, along pathways. The flowers don't last long when cut, but I gather small bouquets anyway because of the delicious fragrance they yield in the warmth of the house. The bulbs are good choices for pot culture too, but keep the plants as cool as possible during their prebloom and blooming stage indoors. In the garden, give the 37

Danford iris a well-drained soil, full sun and a sheltered spot for earliest bloom. Plantings will perennialize best in sites that remain relatively dry in summer. Plant 4 inches apart and 4 inches deep.

The miniature violet-scented iris (*Iris reticulata*), deep violet with a bright orange crest, begins to bloom as the Danford iris is fading. The dark flowers show up best against a light background provided by such flowers as the miniature narcissus 'Tête à Tête,' *Narcissus lobularis* (Lent lily) or 'Yellow Mammoth' crocus. I've situated some plantings in sunny nooks against white boulders. *Iris reticulata* 'Harmony' is a clear sky-blue cultivar with a sparkling yellow crest. Culture is the same as for the Danford iris. Mulch for the winter in zones 3 to 5. Growing these miniature bulbous irises in pots, either sunk outside and brought in when the plants are in bud or forced in the usual way, allows for full savouring of the blooms and their sweet fragrance. All miniature irises produce

slim foliage that grows taller than the flower stems following bloom.

Leucojum spp

(snowflake)

Each slender 16-inch stem of *Leucojum aestivum*, summer snowflake, bears as many as eight nodding white bells with exquisite green edging. Its bloom time and delicate habit make it a natural for contrasting with tulips in the garden, and it is also a fine candidate for naturalizing under trees and among shrubs. For long-term naturalizing, give the bulbs a sunny site with a moist but well-drained soil that is generously supplied with humus. Add an enriching mulch layer of compost and peat moss for the summer, after bloom. The plants supply unusual but attractive cut flowers. Set the bulbs 4 inches apart and 4 inches deep.

The diminutive spring snowflake (*Leucojum vernum*) is pretty at the front of

flowerbeds, in rock gardens and in pots. Culture is the same as for *L. aestivum*.

Muscari spp

(grape hyacinth)

Grape hyacinths are the ultimate in hardy, low-maintenance, multipurpose spring bulbs. Plantings naturalize easily and are long-lived, providing thick carpets of grassy foliage and slender 8-inch flower stems like those of mini-hyacinths. The foliage reappears in late summer or early autumn.

Muscari armeniacum bears slender, deep blue flower spikes and is the most commonly grown cultivar. A gorgeous and equally easy form of the Armenian grape hyacinth is 'Blue Spike,' which forms fat, softly rounded pyramids of fully double, clear blue flowers. This one never fails to arouse comment from visitors to my garden. *M. tubergenianum* is the 'Oxford and Cambridge' muscari, named for the clear bright blue at the top of the flower spikes and the deep Oxford blue below. There is a white form of grape hyacinth also.

Their easygoing nature makes grape hyacinths suitable for just about any free space in the garden. I use them a fair bit for edging, alone or in combination with *Anemone blanda* 'White Splendour.' The bulbs are also well placed in the rock garden, among shrubs and under trees. Grape hyacinths are good subjects for pot culture and are so undemanding that they will continue to bloom for several years in the same pot. This is a bulb that I often transplant in sections from garden to pots for a reliably attractive display in window and fence boxes combined with potted pink or orange primroses. I pot the grape hyacinth plants when they are in bud. In the garden, plant the bulbs 3 inches apart and 4 inches deep. Dead-head by running your fingers up the flower stem, stripping off the spent blooms.

Narcissus spp

(daffodil)

For most of us, the fresh, sweet scents and sunny hues of the daffodil symbolize springtime more powerfully than any other bulb. But the large, golden trumpet daffodils most commonly grown in home gardens and sold as cut flowers are only a small representation of a remarkably varied flower. From the tiniest miniature to the most statuesque cultivar, there is a daffodil for every pot, for just about every garden situation and for each personal preference in flower style.

If you have ever wondered which among the names "daffodil," "narcissus" and "jonquil" is correct, it has in the past been common practice to use the term daffodil for the larger trumpet and large-cupped kinds, the most familiar ones. Narcissus was reserved for the less commonly known smaller-flowered and bunch-flowered types. Although the botanical name 39 for all of them is *Narcissus*, the common and popular term daffodil is becoming recognized for all these flowers, and I have no qualms about using this name. The jonquils constitute a particular class of daffodil characterized by reedlike foliage, two or three flowers per stem and an intensely sweet fragrance. Whatever the name, all are faithful spring bloomers.

Because daffodil cultivars have become so numerous with extensive breeding, they have been classified into divisions according to the plant's heritage and the shape of the flower. A full description belongs in a book devoted solely to bulbs, but a brief sorting-out may be helpful. All of the divisions contain many familiar cultivars along with some stunning new ones (names in parentheses below), and some of the divisions are given self-explanatory titles: division 1, Trumpets ('King Alfred,' 'Golden Harvest,' 'Unsurpassable'); 2, Large Cups ('Carlton,' 'Professor Einstein'); 3, Small Cups ('Barrett Browning'); 4, Double Flowers ('White Lion,' 'Tahiti'). Plants in divisions 1 to 4 have the larger, showier blooms of the daffodil tribe, with one flower on each stem. The ruffled and twisted centres of double flowers are often so heavy that they need support in rain or at least some mulch to protect them from spattering.

The next group of divisions – 5, Triandrus; 6, Cyclamineus; 7, Jonquilla; 8, Tazetta; and 9, Poeticus – is made up of generally shorter plants, with a range of 6- to 16-inch stems and several blossoms on each stem. Many of these daffodils are excellent candidates for indoor pot culture, cut flowers, rock gardens or front-of-border sites.

Division 10 contains all the species and wild forms; all are short-stemmed, and though a few have large flowers, most are tiny, dainty-flowered delights that deserve to be placed where they can be appreciated and not engulfed by nearby plantings. They want full sun and a perfectly drained soil. Division 11, Split Cups, includes intriguing flowers with ruffled cups, split open and laid back over the petals.

While miniature daffodils are best in intimate settings, the tall-stemmed ones provide splashes of colour between dark evergreens, amid ground covers such as ivies or with perennials whose growing foliage disguises their own languishing leaves after bloom. They may be combined with birch clumps, scarlet tulips or a drift of blue grape hyacinths.

Daffodils naturalize easily in grassy areas, in open woodland and within flower and shrub beds. To perennialize well, they do need sun to ripen the foliage during at least a six-week period following bloom. Plant only in grassy areas that are not cut during that time. For long-term naturalizing, give the bulbs a generous spacing of 6 to 8 inches apart and a site where the soil remains dryish during the summer. Otherwise, plant the large bulbs 5 inches apart and 8 inches deep. The smaller bulbs of species and miniatures are spaced 4 inches apart and 4 inches deep. Plant daffodils as early as possible, and move any bulbs whose sites you wish to shift as soon as the foliage has died down. They can be directly set in their new location if it is free, as they commonly begin sending out their new roots as early as the latter part of July – an indication of how soon daffodils prefer to begin a new cycle of growth. They are lovely as cut flowers, and most are well suited to growing in pots for living bouquets indoors.

Ornithogalum umbellatum

(star of Bethlehem)

This bulb multiplies with ease, forming neat mounds of grassy foliage with many 8-inch flower stems bearing flat clusters of starry white flowers. I'm partial to using this flower at the base of climbing and tall shrub roses, though it fits virtually anywhere in the garden and is just about care-free. This is a bulb to plant in difficult spots, as it appears to prosper no matter what. Star of Bethlehem is also pretty in pots. Plant 4 inches apart for a quick show in the garden, 6 to 8 inches apart for

long-term naturalizing. Set the bulbs 4 inches deep.

Puschkinia libanotica

(striped squill, Lebanon squill)

This tough, hardy bulb produces 6-inch stems bearing loose clusters of white flowers finely striped with blue. Good for rock gardens, grassy areas, the front of flowerbeds and pots, puschkinia will flower undisturbed for many years in the garden. Plant bulbs 3 inches apart and 4 inches deep.

Scilla spp

(squills, bluebells)

Each bulb of Siberian squill (*Scilla sibirica*) produces strap-shaped leaves and several stems bearing nodding, ballerina- 41

apart for long-term naturalizing, and set the bulbs 4 inches deep.

Tulipa spp

(tulip)

Whenever I think of gardeners in cold climates or call to mind the gardening I've done in colder zones, I am glad there are tulips. The tulip brings to our gardens not only hardiness but an image-stretching array of flower shapes, plant heights and bold, vibrant hues of almost every colour. Because the sizes and styles of tulips are so many and varied, it is possible to find the perfect type for almost any garden situation. Most modern tulips need to be dug and divided every two or three years, although some will last longer. If you want tulips that you don't need to dig very often, look for cultivars recommended for perennialization.

The vast assortment of tulips can make the selection of cultivars for pots and garden a mind-boggling process. Thankfully, a classification system for tulips has sorted them out for us according to time of bloom, parentage and flower form. As with daffodils, a bulb book would cover it all; but a brief, summarized list makes a start. For early flowering, look for Single Early (12 to 16 inches) or Double Early (12 inches) cultivars. In the midseason range are Triumph (16 to 20 inches) and Darwin Hybrids (24 inches). Among late tulips are Single Late (long-stemmed and large-flowered) and Bouquet (three to six branches from a central stem, each with its own flower), Lily-Flowered (22 inches, pointed arching tips on the blooms), Fringed (24 inches, feathered and fringed petal edges), Viridiflora (24 inches, outer petals diffused with green), Rembrandt (virus-caused markings), Parrot (large, flamboyant blooms with waved, twisted and fringed petals) and Double Late, or peony-flowered, tulips.

This brings us to the species tulips and their hybrids – that is, all the wild plants,

skirt bells in a most vivacious blue – a hue that combines wonderfully with early daffodils and tulips. 'Spring Beauty' is the cultivar with the largest flowers and richest colour. There is also a white form, nice to combine with blue squills. *S. tubergeniana* is a delicate light blue with darker stripes, rather like puschkinia. The early spring squills are lovely in pots and naturalize easily in the garden if left undisturbed. These are useful, sprightly early flowers for edgings, rock gardens, the front of flowerbeds and under spring-flowering shrubs and trees. The 6-inch stems provide fine miniature cut flowers. Plant 4 inches apart and 4 inches deep.

Spanish bluebells (*Scilla campanulata*) grow like tall (12- to 18-inch), loose hyacinths with nodding tubular bells in white, blue or pink. Colour mixtures are also available. Where hardy, they are excellent for naturalizing in pockets of the flower garden or in lightly shaded woodland. Plantings are pleasantly located along pathways and under spring-flowering trees. Plant 4 inches apart, or 6 inches

their cultivars and the hybrids developed from them which still retain the characteristics of the original tulip species. Among these are Kaufmanniana, also called water-lily tulips for their large flowers that open wide to greet the spring sunshine, inaugurating the tulip season with bright, low-growing flowers borne above broad, ground-hugging foliage. Because of their early appearance and short stature (6 inches), these tulips make delightful edgings to beds and flowering collars around shrubs, perennials and trees. Fosterana, flowering soon after the Kaufmannianas, is a class of tulips distinctive for a glistening sheen to the blooms. Greigii tulips, which flower about two weeks later, are noted for their large, vividly coloured flowers and broad leaves mottled or striped with brown or purple. They grow about 10 inches tall and combine nicely with grape hyacinths. Finally, Species, or Botanicals, their cultivars and hybrids – the original wild tulips and their improved cultivars – are interesting not only for their historic value but also for their simple beauty, the diminutive stature of most and their ability to perennialize in congenial conditions. Besides, these are fascinating conversation pieces.

Unlike the large-flowered hybrids, which are usually at their best the first year in the garden, the species tulips improve with age as they settle in and colonize. These little tulips have some special needs: they must have full sun and a fast-draining, light-textured soil that is not very fertile and remains dry in summer. I look for sunny edges of planting areas where the soil is thin and the sprinkler doesn't usually reach. Dryish strips along sunny fencelines and beside concrete paths and driveways provide more promising sites. For these tulip fancier's delights, close-up viewing is another must. I've found the species tulips to be something of an addiction – try one, become enchanted, and you're hooked.

The early, low-growing tulips are the easiest to slip into little spots and corners of the garden. The species tulips provide permanent spring flowers in rock gardens and at the edges of ornamental plots. Kaufmanniana, Greigii and Double Early tulips are also good spring edging flowers and are effective grouped in pockets between shrubs. Midseason tulips also fit well in such spaces, though they are spectacular, too, arranged in special spring display beds. The majestic late tulips are best displayed in flowerbed areas of their own. As a general rule, early-to-midseason tulips and short tulips are fine for growing in pots and any that have long enough stems are excellent for cut-flower arrangements.

Plant the largest cultivars 5 inches apart and 8 inches deep, the Early Singles and Doubles 4 inches apart and 6 inches deep and the species tulips 4 inches apart and 5 inches deep.

Helen Chesnut gardens on a half acre in Qualicum Beach, British Columbia, where she works as a freelance writer and daily garden columnist for two British Columbia newspapers.

By Karan Davis Cutler

pring perennials are modest flowers, which is probably why they are often overlooked. Theirs are not the titanic blooms of summer – dahlias the size of dinner plates, peonies like grapefruits. Nor can they compete with many of spring's bulbs – tulips on the scale of brandy snifters and quadruple-ruffled tricoloured jonquils. ✑ But modesty is still a virtue, though more praised during the 19th century than the 20th. Not every flower, as noted American garden writer Katharine S. White sensibly declared, needs to be bigger or double or multihued or fringed or crinkled because of the perpetual "onward and upward" inclinations of the plant industry. Spring's unassuming perennials have many virtues of their own. ✑ Perhaps it is because they are among the first to bloom after my northern garden has been encased in snow and ice for five months that their colours seem particularly intense. The flowers of the Virginia bluebell (*Mertensia virginica*) are as pure and penetrating as the blue of any delphinium (or any ethereal sky, for that matter), and the burning violet of the pasque flower (*Anemone pulsatilla*), sheathed in soft grey, boldly lives up to its name's Latin root *pulso*, which means "to strike." ✑ The blossoms and foliage of spring perennials are captivating enough to stand alone in both woodland and spring gardens, creating a garden within a garden. They also work well 45 as part of larger mixed beds and borders in designs laid out to flower throughout the growing season. Beyond their intrinsic loveliness (and gardeners scarcely have to be convinced by Emerson that "beauty is its own excuse for being"), early perennials are highly practical plants.

Above all, perennials enhance spring's main event, the flowering bulbs. As the supporting cast, they not only guide our eye toward these showy headliners but embellish and enlarge upon their performance as well. They fill out the "living picture," to use English gardener Gertrude Jekyll's term, making it "soul-satisfying" by contributing dissimilar shapes, colours and textures, by shading and by accenting as companions, underplantings and backdrops.

There is great variety among spring perennials: there are plants with small, delicate blooms – the wildflowers bloodroot (*Sanguinaria canadensis*) and hepatica (*Hepatica americana*) are two examples – as well as showier plants like basket-of-gold (*Aurinia saxatilis*), whose sheets of bloom contrast sharply with the usual one-flower-per-plant arrangement of spring bulbs. And there are real differences among the blossom forms themselves: symmetrical arrangements as well as irregular flowers with petals that are dissimilar in shape, size or colour.

While many spring perennials creep along the soil – moss pinks (*Phlox subulata*) come to mind – there are also taller plants such as bleeding heart (*Dicentra spectabilis*) and fernleaf peony (*Paeonia tenuifolia*). Overall, though, spring perennials are a low, rather informal group of plants, less upright and rigid than the tulips and hyacinths they accompany. They are plants that bend with the breeze rather than break in it.

They also offer prettier foliage than the typical basal, entire leaves of most spring bulbs, leaves as dull as the flowers are brilliant. Spring perennials, by contrast, have leaves with all sorts of shapes and leaflets

Bloodroot's strong leaves and delicate blooms show the diversity of spring perennials.

with wonderful technical names like cordate, deltoid, orbicular and spatulate. Even leaf tips have names – aristate, cirrose, obcordate – as do leaf bases – attenuate, hastate, sagittate and more. A few terms are worth learning just to use with pretentious acquaintances. Bloodroot, for instance, has palmate leaves (think of a spread-fingered hand) that are cleft at the apex.

The foliage also varies in its arrangement. Many plants have stem leaves growing in alternate, opposite and whorled arrangements. Perennials additionally depart from the predictable swordlike leaves of bulbous plants in their leaf textures and shadings of green: dark and light, shiny and dull, hairy and smooth and all things in between. They may be variegated with two or more colours. Finally, the foliage of most spring perennials lasts well into the summer. In the process, it cloaks the drying and dying foliage of spring bulbs and provides companionship for later-blooming plants.

Perennials Defined

All plants that live for three or more years are perennials. These include trees and shrubs. But gardeners, when they talk and write about perennials, usually mean herbaceous plants, flowering species with fleshy stems that typically die back in winter but whose roots remain alive to produce new growth in the spring. This world of plants, wrote 19th-century American philosopher John Fiske, "with its magician, chlorophyll, conjuring with sunbeams, is ceaselessly at work bringing life out of death."

Most perennials are permanent plants, rugged and long-lived. Some, such as peonies (*Paeonia* spp), will likely outlive the gardener who plants them. Not all perennials, however, last that long. Recently, a perennial was redefined by two witty garden writers as "any plant which, had it lived, would have bloomed year after year." There are irresistible species, like the pale yellow *Aquilegia chrysantha*, that simply die after two or three years. At least mine do. But most perennials do not die so soon. Those that have been selectively bred may be especially dependable. They return year after year, as faithful as red-winged blackbirds and spring training and all the other signs that assure us of life's recurrent nature.

While annuals – plants that bloom, produce seed and die in a single growing season – have been the focus of many plant breeders, perennials haven't gone without attention either. The development of triploid cultivars – plants with a greater-than-normal number of chromosomes and therefore increased vigour and flower size – is a good example of breeders' skills that are currently being applied to perennial species.

It would be foolish for gardeners to turn their backs on these developments, to not purchase varieties that are resistant to disease or that bloom in clearer, sharper colours. Vita Sackville-West, a British writer and gardener, recommended planting the "best things . . . and only the best forms of the best things, by which I mean that everything should be choice and chosen." At the same time, Sackville-West

Perennials are plants such as bleeding hearts that live for three or more years.

was a fierce defender of growing wild species and old cultivars, many of which continue to be sold because they still have exceptional qualities.

The usual sources of perennial plants are local nurseries, catalogues, friends and the wild. Prices can vary considerably, so I make comparisons before I buy. The selection at local garden centres is often limited; the choice by mail is usually much better, particularly from specialized seed and plant companies. Other gardeners are a wonderful source of plants – gardeners are a generous lot. And occasionally, plants can also be dug in the wild (but check for local restrictions first). Though I always carry a spade in my car trunk, I never dig a wild plant unless I know the species is absolutely endemic to the area and I have a fit spot in my garden to replant it. Never trespass, never dig an endangered or rare species, and never take more than one-quarter of a clump of 47

Gardeners who can reproduce the natural environment of their immediate area may try growing native wildflowers, likely including at least one species of violet.

wild plants. But if you are digging just ahead of a developer's bulldozer or a road crew's grader, take everything you can.

Wildflower Garden

Growing wildflowers is working with nature in a special way. There are thousands of native species from which to choose, including hundreds and hundreds of choice spring-blooming plants. Some have blossoms that are hardly noticeable, but others are as colourful and showy as any hybrid. The catch is that wildflowers, especially spring-flowering woodland varieties, are likely to thrive only in environments closely matching their wild homes.

While many wildflowers can be incorporated successfully into a perennial garden – some so successfully that we no longer think of them as wildflowers – I maintain a separate garden for spring wildflowers, shaded and framed by beech trees. I grow woodland plants native to northern Vermont. The white flowers alone make quite a list: Canada mayflower (*Maianthemum canadense*), starry false Solomon's seal (*Smilacina stellata*), several species of trillium, rue anemone (*Anemonella thalictroides*), wood anemone (*Anemone quinquefolia*), mayapple (*Podophyllum peltatum*), Solomon's seal (*Polygonatum biflorum*), twinleaf (*Jeffersonia diphylla*), squirrel corn (*Dicentra canadensis*), bloodroot (*Sanguinaria canadensis*), foamflower (*Tiarella cordifolia*), starflower (*Trientalis borealis*).

There are other colours, of course, and other favourites. I look forward to the coltsfoot (*Tussilago farfara*) that grows along the dirt road near my mailbox. It is the first easily seen wildflower of spring and is at home in sun or shade. Its radiant yellow flowers appear long before its leaves, which explains another of its common names, son before father. Equally

48

shining is the marsh marigold or American cowslip (*Caltha palustris*), a member of the buttercup family. It grows along streams and in wet places, blooming almost as soon as the ice thaws – so early that Indians called it "flower that opens the swamps." The toothed, heart-shaped leaves are waxy and grow larger after the blossoms fade.

If I could grow only one blue flower, it might be Virginia bluebell (*Mertensia virginica*), a glorious wildflower that needs moist, rich soil. Called by Gertrude Jekyll "the very embodiment of the freshness of early spring," its clusters of hanging blue blossoms open from pink buds; the strongly veined, bluish leaves die out during the summer. Violets (*Viola* spp), at least the common blue violet (*V. papilionacea*), never die out. Mine have become a plague, wildly spreading in sun and shade; yet it wouldn't be spring without them. There are cultivated varieties, including the scented *V. odorata* 'Royal Robe,' which have all the charm of the species but reproduce a bit less boldly. One more blue flower – alpine forget-me-not (*Myosotis alpestris*) – is not always reliably perennial for me, but it self-seeds so easily that I am yearly treated to a blue sea under an old apple tree. The sky-coloured flower of *M. scorpioides* has a yellow eye, like a tiny sun. Both species are easy to pull out if they begin to move beyond where they are wanted.

There are many fine books available on wildflowers, as well as nurseries, associations and environmental groups devoted to native plants. Before I add to my garden any of the lovely wild plants that bloom in the spring, I learn everything I can about their culture. It is my small contribution to their survival.

Ferns

Native ferns also prefer a setting similar to the one they enjoy in the wild, but placed properly, they flourish almost un-tended. Handsome and varied, they are wonderfully effective additions to the spring garden. Ferns are flowerless and fruitless, giving rise to an early superstition that the possession of a fern seed bestowed magical powers: "We have the receipt of fernseed, we walk invisible," wrote Shakespeare in *Henry IV*. Entirely green, ferns can serve as accents, but they also mix well with other plants, providing backdrops for shorter ones and punctuation between colours. As the delicate yet vigorous fronds unfurl, they conceal the decaying foliage of spring bulbs.

Garden encyclopaedias detail the requirements of particular species. In general, ferns need partial shade and slightly acidic soil that is rich in humus and evenly moist. They can be propagated most easily by division. The common, five-fingered or maidenhair fern (*Adiantum pedatum*), with its nearly black stems and flat-spreading fronds, is one of the loveliest early ferns, but it is slow to spread, must be grown in very moist soil and is more difficult to cultivate than most species. The lady fern (*Athyrium filix-femina*) is far simpler to grow and will tolerate a good deal of sun. The finely cut hay-scented fern (*Dennstaedtia punctilobula*) is among my favourites. It spreads almost too easily, tolerates drought well and can be grown in sunny locations as well as in light shade. Also valuable are wood ferns (*Dryopteris* spp), which have finely cut, feathered leaflets and prefer shaded settings, and the Christmas fern (*Polystichum acrostichoides*), which is evergreen and useful for cutting.

Most of these ferns grow less than three feet high, but there are also tall varieties. The ostrich fern (*Matteuccia struthiopteris*) can reach five feet and is best suited to wet locations. It and the much smaller New York fern (*Thelypteris noveboracensis*) are among the most hardy fern species. The cinnamon fern (*Osmunda cinnamomea*) is not particular about soil but likes wet locations and semishade, as do the acid- 49 loving royal fern (*O. regalis*) and a third member of the genus, the interrupted fern (*O. claytoniana*).

Some ferns tolerate limestone soils, including maidenhair spleenwort (*Asplenium trichomanes*) and glade fern (*Athyrium pycnocarpon*). Brake fern or bracken (*Pteridium aquilinum*) will grow in alkaline or acid soil, but it is too invasive for most gardens, as is the sensitive fern (*Onoclea sensibilis*), which thrives in sun or shade.

More Foliage

There are other plants that may be thought of as part of the spring garden, although they bloom much later in the season. Woven among spring bulbs and perennials, they enrich the garden fabric with more varied colour and form. Ornamental grasses, many of which flower in July and August, are examples of summer plants that add interest in the spring.

Among the summer-flowering perennials are several that are grown for their foliage. Lamb's ear (*Stachys lanata*), whose leaves are silver-green, thick and woolly, thrives in full sun. It grows about 8 inches tall and spreads easily. Artemisia is another silver-green foliage plant for full sun. The 12-inch *Artemisia schmidtiana* 'Silver Mound' is the most familiar, but there are varieties as tall as four feet. There is also bishop's weed, or goutweed (*Aegopodium podagraria*), but be warned that it is an enthusiastic traveller, too enthusiastic to be introduced into most gardens. The green and white form *variegatum* is the one to plant and then probably only as a ground cover in a location far removed from other plants. *Lamium maculatum* 'Beacon Silver' is another low-growing foliage plant with silver leaves.

Some of the meadow rues (*Thalictrum* spp) rise four feet and more. The leaves of the shadow-loving early meadow rue (*T. dioicum*) are reminiscent of columbine; other species have less rounded foliage but are just as delicate and attractive. Also cultivated for its foliage is hosta. There are hundreds of varieties: large, small, variegated, veined, margined, puckered and coloured in shades of green, grey and blue. Among my favourite cultivars are the eight-inch 'Blue Moon,' the foot-tall 'Blue Wedgwood,' the classic, gold-edged 'Frances Williams' and 'Blue Umbrellas,' rightfully called "a landscape powerhouse" by one nursery catalogue.

Still another group of plants consists of the stonecrops (*Sedum* spp). Members of a huge genus of great variety that tends to spread quickly, they flourish in full sun and dry, poor soil. Most species bloom in the summer and fall, but their succulent foliage stands out in the spring garden.

The spring garden can also take advantage of the foliage of early-rising perennials grown for their summer flowers – astilbe, lupin, peony, day lily, Siberian iris and bearded iris, hardy geranium (cranesbill) and ligularia – as well as annuals that have been started indoors.

Site Selection

Garden location is part function, part aesthetics and part necessity. Gardeners place gardens and plants where they fit their purposes, where they "have" to go and where they look beautiful. In 1899, Reynolds Hole, Anglican dean and ardent rosarian, asked friends about the purpose of a garden. Their replies included croquet, garden parties, lawn tennis and botanical research. Twentieth-century responses would differ but slightly. The question of what the garden is for is the first issue gardeners must address, and the answer controls where and what one plants.

Part of my family, for example, still needs room to kick soccer balls and play badminton. Any encroachment – what my husband terms "creeping gardenism" – on our largest open spaces is out of the question. So my garden-making remains

Moisture lovers like ostrich ferns and marsh marigolds redeem an incurably wet site.

other factor: wind can play havoc with delicate blossoms, especially those bold enough to flower in early spring.

Drainage is also crucial: only bog plants and frogs thrive in a swamp, and few from either of those categories are appropriate in most gardens. But there are plants that thrive in wet soil, as well as species that tolerate near-drought conditions; most garden encyclopaedias include lists of each. Finally, if the region's soil is acutely acidic or alkaline, there is little point in battling the chemical realities by planting inappropriate species. Woodland wildflowers simply will not prosper in soil that turns litmus paper blue.

After function is resolved and necessity acknowledged, aesthetics becomes the important concern. Perennials deserve to be placed where they can be seen easily and constantly, where they can be admired and shown off, and where they look their best and add to the overall design of the property. I think flowers, especially smaller perennials, are enhanced by some kind of frame or background, even a meagre one. Not that one must break the bank building fences and walls, though fences and walls are lovely. Conifers, deciduous hedges, vines, shrubs, ferns, even buildings and their masonry foundations can make fine backdrops.

Leave space, at least a couple of feet, between backdrops and plantings. Those two dozen inches allow air circulation and decrease competition between root systems if the backdrop is a live one. Moreover, concrete building foundations are notorious for leaching lime into the soil, often creating conditions that are inhospitable to many plants. And keep in mind that not every straight edge, living or built, needs to be lined with perennials.

Whether free-form or rigidly geometric, beds and borders should be wide enough to permit more than two rows of plants; the usual recommendation is a minimum of 5 feet. I inherited a narrow perennial border, less than 3 feet wide, which

largely on the edges of the lawns and along fences and foundations. For now.

Necessity is also a deciding factor in location, especially in my Vermont garden, which lies atop a solid ledge that sometimes runs only an inch or two below the soil surface. It is a geological reality that dictates absolutely, since I do not resort to heavy machinery or dynamite in order to plant perennials or anything else.

There are other necessities as well. Most cultivated flowers do best in full sunlight. There are exceptions, of course, and a good many of them are spring bloomers such as pulmonaria and bleeding heart. While they thrive in sun in early spring before tree leaves unfurl, they want more shaded conditions once hot weather arrives. Not many perennials thrive in truly deep shade, however, so the amount of light available is a prime consideration when locating flower borders and beds and when choosing plants. Exposure is an-

separates a stone path from the brick base of my small greenhouse. In it, I have spring flowers in front with taller summer perennials behind. It is not on the scale of a Gertrude Jekyll garden with borders 10 feet wide and 50 feet long—few gardens are on that scale any more—but it is lovely. Nonetheless, gardens deep enough to accommodate more than two bands of plants are preferable, especially if you want more than one season of bloom.

Before settling on a design or choosing plants, visit public and private gardens in your area to see what species do well and how other people place and combine them. Read garden books, subscribe to garden magazines and send for every seed and nursery catalogue you can. It is foolish not to capitalize on the experience of others, but it is also entirely acceptable to defy the rules and experiment—only, however, if you can tolerate the I-told-you-so looks when you fail and can control your ego when your impertinence pays off.

Soil

The importance of first-rate soil cannot be overemphasized. "The best ground in the Summer time," wrote Englishman Thomas Hill in 1577, "is neither very drie, nor clayie, nor sandy and rough, nor endamaged with gapings, procured by the heat of Summer." His observation is as good today as it was 400 years ago. Since it is the roots that not only maintain perennials from year to year but often spread and produce new plants, soil conditions that encourage healthy roots are a prerequisite for success.

Good root development requires soil that both drains well and retains moisture, conditions that may seem to be at cross-purposes. They are not, however, and are characteristic of soil that is rich in organic material, or humus. It is possible to enrich the soil of an established perennial garden, but it is very difficult, though not impossible, to change its soil structure.

Adding organic matter—peat moss, compost, animal manure, sawdust, leaf mould—to the soil is the best way to improve its structure. Humus makes sandy soil more water-retentive and opens up clay soils. It is almost the gardener's equivalent of Lydia E. Pinkham's Vegetable Compound, the 19th-century cure for women's every ill.

Organic matter does not cure every garden ill, but it does much more for soil than Lydia's compound ever did for women. Most organic materials not only improve the soil structure but also add nutrients and buffer the acidity or alkalinity of the soil in the process. (Peat moss is without nutrient value, but it does increase acidity.) In general, perennials do best in slightly acid soil (pH 6.5); woodland plants, many of which bloom in early spring, prefer a little more acidity (pH 5.5). Area agricultural extension services in the United States and provincial departments of agriculture in Canada can provide information and help in testing soil pH.

If the soil is well prepared and has a high organic content—if the soil itself has been well fed—little additional fertilizer is necessary. If feeding is called for, a good fertilizer ratio (N-P-K) for the perennial garden is 1-2-2 or even 0-2-2. Most perennials do not need great amounts of nitrogen (N), as I learned one year after producing flowerless six-foot Shasta daisies in an over-fertilized plot. Phosphorus (P), the second element in the formula, is important to root and tuber development, to flower and seed production and to disease resistance. Bone meal and ground phosphate rock can supply phosphorus to plants. Potassium (K), the third component, aids fruit production and helps plants ward off disease and tolerate cold temperatures. Wood ash is an excellent source of potash, or potassium oxide, the form of potassium used by plants; other sources are granite dust, seaweed and hay.

Bulbs and perennials thrive with shrubs requiring acidity (rhododendrons and pieris) *in a mature garden where close attention has been given to the soil.*

The Greeks, according to early garden writer Thomas Hill, believed horse manure "the vilest and worst of all dungs," but I add it to my perennial gardens each year. Already mixed with hay and sawdust, it does wonders for my rocky soil. If there were not a natural supply, I might be tempted to follow in the footsteps of a crusty English vicar who grew magnificent roses and flowers but refused to reveal the secret of his success. Finally, cornered by gardeners in the parish, he confessed: "I bury a dead cat under each bush."

Planting, Multiplying

Because early frosts are more often the rule than the exception in northern gardens, most perennials, especially dormant bare-rooted plants and seedlings, should be planted in the spring. Fall planting simply does not allow enough time for the good root development necessary to carry perennials through the winter. Having said that, I confess I often plant spring-flowering species in the late summer or very early fall, knowing that if I delay planting until spring, I may have to wait a year for the first blossoms. This choice requires more work on my part, for until winter, I must ensure that the plant gets adequate moisture and is shaded and mulched. It may also need winter protection.

But dividing and transplanting—including planting potted perennials newly purchased from a nursery—are possible throughout the growing season. As long as plants spend at least a month in the garden before the really cold weather arrives, planting is not so much a question of when but of how. If moved quickly, reset carefully and watered generously, most perennials can be moved or divided any time during the growing season.

Except for fall-blooming species, I divide plants just after they flower. It works well for most perennials, but not all, so it makes sense to read about individual plants before grabbing the spading fork off the wall. Division is the simplest way to propagate perennials, though some species are easier to divide than others. In many cases, after the plant has been dug, a few good shakes will make the clump fall apart into separate plants; pulmonaria and primroses (*Primula* spp) are good examples.

Leopard's bane is an example of a plant that will divide readily in spring or fall.

Other plants, such as day lilies, have roots so intertwined that separating them is a formidable chore. Rather than using two back-to-back spading forks to pry the roots apart, I soak the roots in buckets of water. Once all the dirt is soaked or hosed off, I can see what I am doing, and the roots become fairly easy to untangle. I warn you that this is my own invention; I have never seen it recommended in garden books. I don't think I've ever lost a day lily, but that may be a testimonial to their hardiness rather than to my method. Still, I often soak clumps of perennials before I divide them, finding that it both hydrates the plants and reduces the tearing and breaking of their roots.

Some perennials have to be broken or cut apart. Iris and astilbe are examples of ornamentals that just don't cooperate in separating on their own. I use a sharp, clean knife to cut the clumps into sections, taking care to leave several buds or eyes on each division. When I'm rushed or feeling lazy, I sometimes make divisions by cutting into the clump with a spade and removing a section, without lifting the entire plant. This technique, most often recommended for shallow-rooted perennials like lamb's ears (*Stachys lanata*) and bee balm (*Monarda didyma*), is best used on less delicate species.

A very few plants, such as columbines (*Aquilegia* spp), are nearly impossible to divide. Most perennials, however, are easy to separate and do not have to be treated cautiously. But gentleness is important when replanting and caring for the divisions. Once the clump is separated, I cut the foliage back, halfway or a little more (but *not* completely off), to reduce water loss. Next, I soak the divisions for several hours in water and then immediately reset them at the proper depth, usually the depth at which they were already growing. New divisions need ample space for their roots, organically rich soil that is firmed carefully so that no air remains around the roots, and plenty of moisture. I give reset plants shade for a week or so, mulch them and use evergreen boughs to protect them during their first winter. I also mark where I've set the divisions so that I won't accidentally dig into them in the spring.

Most garden books provide tables of how often perennials should be divided. No plant has to be divided unless it is overrunning its neighbours or no longer has the growing space it needs. Plants without good light, sufficient air circulation or enough root room are easy prey for disease and are likely to lose vigour. In my experience, perennials need division far less frequently than experts usually recommend; but if the plant looks less healthy

While many perennials are easy to divide, a few, like columbines, are difficult.

Garden encyclopaedias recommend the best ways to propagate specific varieties. Whatever the method, propagating perennials means an exponential increase in plants, not just an arithmetic one. But gardening, as May Sarton declares in *Plant Dreaming Deep*, is "a grand passion. It seizes a person whole . . . and he [or she] soon learns that a garden is an ever-expanding venture." Especially a perennial garden.

Routine Care

Perennial gardens are repeatedly tagged as "care-free" and "effortless," but don't believe it. "A gardener's work is never at an end," wrote John Evelyn in 1666, and the invention of rotary tillers and chemical pesticides has not nullified his observation. After a perennial garden has been established in well-prepared, fertile soil, there are still regular tasks to be carried out. The more faithfully they are done, the less often some have to be repeated and the closer the garden moves to being easy to maintain – not effortless, by any means, but easy.

It is hard to wait for the soil to warm in spring, but once it begins to heat up, so do the spring garden chores. While my interest and energy are high, I rework every bed and border, first removing any evergreen boughs or mulches I laid down for winter protection, then weeding, cultivating and edging, fertilizing with well-rotted manure and dividing and moving plants. This is also the time, if tests show it is needed, to correct the soil pH. Finally, when the soil is warm, 50 degrees F or so, I mulch with compost mixed with aged sawdust. I also add dried grass clippings from the lawn when they are available. Mulching not only helps to retain moisture but retards weeds and eventually decays and enriches the soil. I am not enthusiastic about the packaged shredded-bark and wood-chip mulches, however – not because of their effectiveness (which is rela-

or is producing few flowers and the heart of the clump is dead, it is time to divide. More critical, if you or a neighbour need more plants, it is time to divide.

Division is not the only propagation method. Perennials can also be multiplied by stem and root cuttings. These methods, which are detailed in garden encyclopaedias, are especially useful when you want more plants but the clump is still too small to divide or is a variety that is difficult to divide. Starting plants from seed takes patience, for it is usually at least a year until the first blossom appears. Some species are relatively easy to start from seed, others are much more difficult, and there is no way of generalizing. But seeds are far less expensive than seedlings or plants, and often, buying seeds is the only way to obtain unusual species and varieties. Any reputable seed house provides specific germination instructions with each package of seed.

A casual, "natural" garden is less likely to be due to nature than to the gardener's vision, selectivity and knowledge of what goes well with what.

tively good) but because they are expensive, take forever to decompose and are not very attractive. Judging from their popularity, my view is not the majority's.

Another job that comes early in the season is staking. Happily, most spring perennials don't need staking, and I hate the task so much that I do not grow any species that do. But if there are plants in the garden that will require support, find the least obvious method and do it early. Nothing looks worse than a plant that has been allowed to sag and sprawl and then is trussed and resurrected.

If the soil is mulched and rich in organic matter, watering shouldn't be much of a job, except in drought years or in regions that typically receive little rainfall. Plants vary in the amount of water they need; the rule of thumb is an inch of water per week. Shallow-rooted plants, such as pulmonaria and primula, are the most susceptible to lack of rain. Newly planted or transplanted perennials also need constant moisture.

Once gardens have undergone spring cleaning, maintenance becomes routine. I try to keep on top of things by checking each bed or border weekly. On my rounds, I weed, dead-head, prune and check for insects and diseases. These routine trips into the garden are also good opportunities to look at the garden's design, to see combinations that are pleasing or could be changed and to notice plants that need division or relocation. Among my recent notes are: "Once and for all, get rid of that damn purple coneflower" and "The pulmonaria next to the pink azalea is wonderful: divide it."

By providing the cleanest and best growing conditions I can, I grow healthy, strong plants and also avoid many insect and disease problems. And because I want not only blossoms but also butterflies, bees, toads, ladybugs, hummingbirds and most of their friends in my garden, I almost never use commercial insecticides or fungicides. If a particular species or variety repeatedly attracts insects or is bothered by disease, I either seek out a better strain, one bred for resistance, or stop growing it altogether.

Once perennial foliage dies back – late summer for many spring-blooming species – I cut it down to the ground, adding the dried stalks to my compost pile. Old stems and leaves are the ideal winter habitat for insects and diseases. Last, when the soil has frozen solid, I mulch with compost and rotted manure and protect less hardy plants or any fall transplants or divisions with pine and hemlock branches. Hay, straw, pine needles, dry leaves and half-made compost are also good for protecting plants. And then I begin planning for spring.

"Gardening is largely a question of mixing one sort of plant with another sort of plant," wrote Vita Sackville-West, and if they don't join happily, then one must be rooted out. "The true gardener must be brutal." Because spring perennials tend to be small plants, many can be included, but even the early garden – the garden that begins with snowdrops and winter aconites and ends with the first chorus of bearded irises, peonies and lupins – must be selective.

Garden columnist Allen Lacy echoes Sackville-West's advice, recommending "a healthy set of prejudices" to help in choosing among the largest group of plants, those "about which controversy is possible." Among the handsome spring flowers I would place in this category are the pasque flower (*Anemone pulsatilla*), which does well for others but not for me; the fernleaf peony (*Paeonia tenuifolia*), which refuses to stand up without support and looks awful when supported; and the dwarf bearded iris (*Iris verna*), whose velvet flowers look too large for their foliage.

But I cannot imagine a spring garden without ferns, a few woodland wildflowers and at least half of the 16 spring peren-

nials listed below – flowers that, in Lacy's words, "only the perverse could dislike."

Aethionema spp

(stone-cress, Persian candytuft)

Garden books too often assign ground-hugging plants such as Persian candytuft exclusively to rock gardens or to service as ground covers. But many of them also belong in mixed borders and beds, where they provide a green carpet all summer and colour all spring with their bloom. Other plants that share these traits with aethionema are *Arabis* spp, *Armeria maritima*, *Asperula odorata*, *Aubrieta deltoidea*

and *Iberis sempervirens*. In spring, Persian candytuft is a mass of small pink flower heads, or umbels, masking the blue-green needlelike foliage that later provides colour and texture to the garden. Aethionema prefers sun and well-drained soil and may need to be mulched in winter.

Alchemilla spp

(lady's mantle)

Lady's mantle is prized for its foliage: wonderful, multilobed, slightly cupped 57

may explain why these lovely perennials quietly fly off after two or three seasons. Yet they are so striking and graceful that regular replanting is acceptable. "No Garden," opined John Parkinson more than three centuries ago, "would willingly be without them."

There are several North American species, including the early-blooming red and yellow *Aquilegia canadensis*, the blue and white rock bells (*A. caerulea*) and the stunning yellow *A. chrysantha*, which was dis-

leaves with serrated margins that catch dew and raindrops and transform them into sparkling cut crystals. The droplets were gathered as medicine by alchemists in the Middle Ages, which explains the plant's scientific name, *Alchemilla mollis* (syn. *A. vulgaris*), a latinized version of the Arabic word for alchemy.

A European native, the shallow-rooted lady's mantle is easily divided and also self-sows readily. Its tiny yellow-green flowers are of only secondary interest. Often used with roses and shrubs, the smaller *Alchemilla alpina* is best for underplanting. Both species go well with ferns and white astilbe, and their foliage contrasts attractively with the spiky leaves of spring bulbs. Despite its appeal to the sophisticated gardener, lady's mantle is a pushover to grow and survives in nearly any location. But it does best in partial shade and average soil, where it maintains its foliage throughout the summer, remaining interesting until the first hard frost.

Aquilegia spp

(columbine)

Both the Latin *Aquilegia* and the English name columbine refer to birds, which

covered in California in 1873. Modern garden types, *A.* x *hybrida*, result from the interbreeding of these natives as well as of European and Asian species. The tall, long-spurred 'McKana Giant' and 'Olympia' strains are among the choicest hybrids and are widely available in an enormous range of colours.

The bell-shaped flowers, which dance above deeply lobed foliage, are formed in combinations of fives: five hollow-centred petals growing backward to form spurs and five inner petal-like sepals. The blooms, often bicoloured and loved by hummingbirds, are long-lasting in bouquets. Columbines are not good flowers for massed plantings but are fine in the mixed border, lovely with wild phlox (*Phlox divaricata*) and superb when accented against a dark backdrop.

Some species prefer full sun, but most garden varieties like semishade and moist, slightly acidic soil. While it is hardy to zone 3, the columbine's penchant for dying out and cross-fertilizing means replanting every few seasons. Fortunately, plants are easy to bring from seed, which American Indians called "black perfume" and used to scent their clothes.

Arabis spp

(rock cress)

Arabis albida (syn. *A. caucasica*) is one of the backbones of the rockery, but I grow it in the front of perennial beds for both its silver-grey leaves and its long-lasting, symmetrical white flowers. There are also double and pink forms. Its slightly fragrant woolly leaves tumble and fill in spaces at bed edges best when it is planted in full sun and rich, well-drained soil. Cut

the plants back after blooming to promote future growth.

Armeria maritima

(thrift, sea-pink)

Another favourite for rock gardens, thrift, or sea-pink, was popular in the Tudor era in the knot gardens so characteristic of that time, and it is still a useful edging plant in any perennial bed. From tight carpets of bluish, grasslike foliage emerge 4-inch wiry stems holding single globular flower heads, rather like chive blossoms; there are white, pink and rose varieties. *Armeria maritima*, a native of the Mediterranean shores, insists on full sun and dry soil.

Asperula odorata

(sweet woodruff)

Sweet woodruff readily forms an elegant ground cover. The plant has a fine white flower, which is star-shaped and held in terminal clusters above dense whorls of green leaves. It prefers partial shade and moist, humus-rich soil. Culti- 59

shade or full sun; it needs plenty of moisture and a well-balanced soil.

Aurinia saxatilis

(basket-of-gold)

Though new to most gardeners, *Aurinia saxatilis* is a perfect name for what we once called *Alyssum saxatile*, for it means "golden" and "growing among the rocks." The country names basket-of-gold and gold dust are equally apt, as its clumps of rosette flowers look like spilt sacks of coins dropped by escaping pirates.

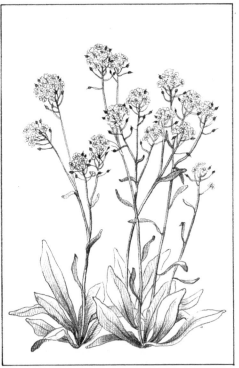

vated in England for more than 600 years, it was valued for its scent – "doth very well attemper the aire," wrote Gerard in 1597 – and is the traditional herb of May wine.

Aubrieta deltoidea

(purple rock cress)

Closely related to the genus *Arabis*, purple rock cress is another rock-garden plant that is also an excellent candidate for the perennial border. The matlike, ground-hugging green (or in some varieties, variegated) foliage is attractive even after the pink-to-violet-to-purple flowers have given their spring display. Cutting back ruthlessly after the blooms fade will keep the plant within bounds. Aubrieta grows easily from seed and can tolerate partial

The lance-shaped foliage, which is hairy and greyish green, grows 6 to 12 inches high. The plant likes to ramble. It should be trimmed back once the flowers fade to avoid legginess. Full sun is essential for compact growth and good bloom. Well-drained soil is also important, especially in northern gardens, though it need be only moderately rich and slightly acidic.

Basket-of-gold is nearly impossible to divide because of its long taproot, but stems will self-root or can be rooted and it is easy to raise from seed. Groups of plants are more successful than one glaring golden clump, and they interplant well with forget-me-nots (*Myosotis sylvatica*). *Aurinia saxatilis* 'Compactum' is a shorter variety, while 'Citrinum' has pale yellow flowers. There are also double varieties.

Bergenia spp

(giant rockfoil)

Although their long-lasting waxy flower clusters are handsome – closely packed on stiff vertical stems in pink, rose and white – it is the rosettes of bergenia's bold foliage that add something different to the spring garden. First discovered in Siberia by a scientific expedition commissioned by Peter the Great, bergenias were once classified as saxifrages.

Renamed for a German botanist, Karl August von Bergen, they grow in basal clumps from thick rhizomes. Heartleaf bergenia (*Bergenia cordifolia*) has broad, fleshy, heart-shaped (cordate) leaves 6 to

8 inches across, which are tinged rose-red in autumn. 'Silverlight,' a white cultivar, blooms especially early; 'Evening Glow' is dark red with purplish green foliage. Leatherleaf bergenia (*B. crassifolia*) is slightly taller (16 inches) and has spoon-shaped, glossy leaves. Its flowers rise well above the leaves.

Both species are hardy, flourish in average soil, tolerate dry as well as wet conditions and prefer a partially sunny location. Best propagated by division, they combine effectively with spring bulbs, especially lavender tulips, and grow well under trees.

Dicentra spp

(bleeding heart)

Dicentra spectabilis, or common bleeding heart, is one of spring's tall perennials. Happily located, well-established clumps can rise 3 feet and live indefinitely. The name bleeding heart, of course, refers to the plant's blossom, which is shaped so unusually that dicentra is also known as lady's locket, Dutchman's breeches and our-lady-in-a-boat. Linnaeus thought the flower resembled the wing cases of an insect.

Both flower and foliage are lovely. The pink and white blooms, often a dozen or more, hang from the arching racemes like charms on a bracelet. The graceful grey-green leaves, which yellow and die in summer, are deeply incised. The fernlike foliage of the fringed, or plumed, bleeding heart (*Dicentra eximia*) is even more finely cut and lasts until frost. This native American species is more compact, less than 15 inches high, and continues to bloom throughout the summer; 'Adrian Bloom' is a fine crimson variety.

All bleeding hearts like moist, light soil enriched with organic matter and need a half-day of sun or filtered shade. Plants can be propagated by division and root cuttings, but the task must be approached carefully because the roots, technically 61

rhizomes, are fragile. Garden books insist that bleeding hearts self-sow, but that hasn't been the case in my garden.

Common bleeding heart is lovely combined with lavender tulips or Jacob's ladder (*Polemonium caeruleum*). I grow a large clump under an aspen, underplanted with *Vinca minor* and lavender crocuses. A stunning photograph led me to white bleeding heart (*Dicentra spectabilis* 'Alba'), which I now grow in combination with *Pulmonaria saccharata* 'Alba,' white tulips and lily-of-the-valley (*Convallaria majalis*). And with unlimited enthusiasm.

Doronicum spp

(leopard's bane)

Doronicum is the season's first daisy. As bright and easy to grow as its summer cousins, this perennial is a fine addition to the spring garden. *Doronicum cordatum* (syn. *D. caucasicum*) is my favourite because of its compact form, but there is also a taller species, *D. plantagineum*, which is good for the back of large borders. Both have cheerful, all-yellow flowers that are excellent for cutting. There is also a double variety, *D. cordatum* 'Spring Beauty,'

but it lacks the simple charm of the single.

Known as leopard's bane because of its legendary use by game hunters as an arrow poison, the plant is very hardy and flourishes in sun or light shade. Plants are easily divided, either in the spring or in August when they are dormant. Doronicum's rough-textured, heart-shaped leaves add interest to the spring garden but disappear in summer, so it should be located near plants like astilbe or hosta, whose

foliage persists until frost. In defiance of that advice, a glorious combination is doronicum and the crimson-and-yellow tulip 'Rembrandt.'

Iberis sempervirens

(evergreen candytuft)

Spring is flush with low-growing perennials, and *Iberis sempervirens*, its 6-inch foliage mounds drenched with clusters of tiny white flowers, is a perfect example. The variety 'Autumn Snow' flowers in spring and then again in the fall. Tough and durable (the name *sempervirens* means always green), candytuft became the Oriental symbol of indifference. It grows in full sun or light shade, likes

neutral soil and should be sheared back after blooming.

Evergreen candytuft can be grown easily from seed sown directly where it will grow. Germination takes two or three weeks.

Phlox spp

(phlox)

In *Colour Schemes for the Flower Garden*, English plantswoman Gertrude Jekyll described her Hidden Garden, which had a bank to the left and a rocky mound to the right. In late May and early June, she wrote, "the glory of the mound is the long stretch of blue-lilac *Phlox divaricata*, whose colour is again repeated by a little of the same on the sunny bank to the left."

There are three native *Phlox* species for the spring garden, but only one, wild phlox (*Phlox divaricata*; syn. *P. canadensis*), resembles the familiar summer varieties. One to two feet tall, wild phlox is slightly fragrant, its five-petalled flowers borne in loose clusters on sticky stalks. The sticky coating traps crawling insects,

thus saving the plant's nectar for butterflies. A pale lilac-blue in the wild, its cultivars also appear in white and lavender. Wild phlox prefers partial shade and organically rich, well-drained soil.

The two other species are both creeping forms. Moss pink (*Phlox subulata*) is suited for full sun and gritty, alkaline soils; creeping phlox (*P. stolonifera*), which blooms slightly later, prefers shade and acidic, humus-rich soil. The fragrant flower clusters of creeping phlox rise above the oval, evergreen leaves that cling close to the ground. Wonderful in informal woodland gardens, creeping phlox spreads on its own but can be propagated by division as well.

Moss pinks, brilliant mats of colour, are among spring's most useful perennials, wonderful for edging, for borders and beds and for rock gardens. Their needle-like foliage is evergreen, eclipsed for a month each spring by scores of flat, five-petalled flowers in colours ranging from white to pink, rose to deep red and pale blue to lavender. The greenery should be sheared halfway back after flowering to promote new growth. Moss pinks love sun and average, well-drained soil; rich soil or shade produces leggy plants. New plants may be propagated by division and stem cuttings, but moss pinks self-root 63 so easily that those methods may not be necessary.

Primula spp

(primrose)

There are nearly as many primroses in literature as there are species in nature and varieties in cultivation. From the hundreds of poetic possibilities, Coleridge's description – "In dewy glades, / The peering primrose, like sudden gladness, / Gleams on the soul . . . " – is among the most apt and characterizes most of the thousands of botanical possibilities.

Nearly all *Primula* species need shade, humus-rich soil and moisture – especially moisture. *P. auricula* types and *P. veris* (cowslips) tolerate sun only if they get enough water. An east-facing location has been ideal for the varieties that brighten my northern garden: *P. auricula*, *P. veris*, *P. vulgaris* and *P.* x *polyantha*. The last originated as a natural cross involving three species and has been of greatest interest to plant breeders and gardeners.

Polyanthus holds its flower clusters on 6-inch stems, well above the tongue-shaped, wrinkled foliage. My favourites are the pale yellows, like 'Old Sulphur Yellow,' but there are colours spanning the rainbow. There are also doubles, double-deckers, bicolours and edged varieties. In cool temperatures, plants bloom for a month or more.

Primroses are best planted in groups and can be used as edging plants in a formal design. They are most at home, however, in a natural setting and blend well with other spring perennials and bulbs. While primroses bloom in colours as brilliant as those of tulips, one of the season's sweetest pictures is pale yellow primroses combined with forget-me-nots (*Myosotis scorpioides*) and hosta.

In Germany, primroses are known as "keys to heaven," while English-speaking people, thanks to Shakespeare and others, travel "the primrose way to the everlasting bonfire." Regardless of one's destination, primroses are friendly companions and among the perennial treasures of early spring.

Pulmonaria spp

(lungwort)

The medicinal-sounding name *Pulmonaria* comes from the Latin word for lung. The name choice is an example of a 16th-century theory called the Doctrine of Signatures, which held that plants that

resembled parts of the body were curatives for those parts. The spotted leaves of pulmonaria were thought to resemble diseased lungs.

The slightly hairy, mottled foliage of *Pulmonaria saccharata*, which grows in basal clumps 6 to 10 inches high and spreads freely by way of underground stems, gives rise to several common names, including Mary's milkdrops and spotted dog. The creamy blotches are irregular and give the effect of patches of light amidst the dark green.

The drooping, tubular blossoms normally change colour as they mature, from pink to blue or pink to rose. The presence of two colours on a single stem has given rise to a host of additional names: Joseph and Mary, Adam and Eve, soldiers and sailors. Among the first perennials to flower, pulmonaria often bloom for a month or longer.

These are not particular plants, but organically rich soil best retains the water their shallow roots need. Without moisture and partial shade, pulmonaria foliage wilts quickly. The plants can be grown under trees and in dark corners and combine well with small pink azaleas or, in cooler climates, yellow and white narcissus.

Vinca minor

(lesser periwinkle)

Only 5 inches tall and often thought of solely as a ground cover for shaded locations, lesser periwinkle or creeping myrtle (*Vinca minor*) is a common companion for spring bulbs. This is a much more cheerful use than the plant was given by the Romans, who fashioned vinca garlands for prisoners about to be executed. Evergreen in northern areas with good snow cover, the plant's dark, glossy foliage underlies lilac-blue flowers that combine well with spring perennials and tall-growing bulbs.

Vinca grows and flowers best in partially shaded, moist, friable soil. Plant runners tend to self-root; summer stem cuttings root easily too, and plants, which should be spaced a foot apart, can also be divided. There are double, plum- and white-coloured forms, as well as plants with variegated leaves, but they tend to be less hardy than the widely available blue form.

While it is an interesting addition to perennial gardens, vinca must be kept within bounds. It spreads moderately fast, but once plants become well established, their strong stems weave a mat that other plants may be unable to penetrate. Fittingly, "the leaves of periwinkle eaten by man and wife together" would, according to Culpeper, weave them together in love.

Karan Davis Cutler, garden columnist for two Vermont newspapers, freelance writer for several journals and full-time librarian, has gardened in northern Ohio and Vermont.

Chapter Four:
Spring-Flowering Shrubs

By Brenda Cole

I f trees are the skeleton of the garden, shrubs are surely the flesh, rounding out the corners and giving shape to the plantings. "We must cover the bones with flesh and breathe life into [them], each according to his skill and imagination," wrote Francis Kingdon Ward in *The Romance of Gardening* (1935). "When it comes to growing plants, every man must write his own book of experience." Famous for his plant explorations in China and eastern Asia, Ward recognized the value of long-established, nonnative shrubs familiar to his readers. "Who, for example, does not know the common lilac, an alien from the Balkans . . . better than he knows the English wayfaring tree! . . . We have always encouraged Free Trade amongst foreign plants, to the lasting benefit of our country." And so in the list of shrubs that follows, there are many "foreign plants," sometimes closely related to our native species but better able to withstand the rigours of city life and confined spaces. ◌ Shrub or tree – where is the line drawn? In general, a plant with a single stem is classed as a tree, while the same plant branching from below ground level is considered a shrub. But the line is fuzzy. The white birch, though frequently growing in multi-trunk clumps, is still considered a tree; and when, not too commonly, shrubs are grown as specimen plants without companion competition, any of the taller 67

Shrubs such as azaleas play a part in the garden that bursts into glory with the beginning of spring and yet maintains its structure all year round.

species, such as the Saskatoon or hybrid lilacs, may attain small-tree dimensions. Many woody plants are available in either form. Rather like children, the way they are treated when young determines the way they will turn out.

Shrubs play many roles in the garden. Frequently, they are used to hide things — the concrete foundation of the house, the corner with the compost heap, a view of junked cars or simply the neighbour's garden. In this they excel, for not only will carefully chosen species or varieties grow rapidly to fill the desired spaces, but their rate of growth will also slow once they have reached the desired height.

Another way of growing shrubs to blank out an unwanted view or give privacy is to organize them into trimmed hedges in a more formal design plan. Some shrubs accept this well, but those whose glory lies in their flowers and fruit will hardly have a chance to produce ei-

ther. A gentler formal treatment, the training of shrubs against a wall in some form of espalier, will allow blooming and fruiting, as the plants are carefully pruned rather than trimmed — but this does require a skilled hand.

More popular, and more commonly grown, is the looser, informal border where a variety of shrubs, subjected to a minimum of necessary trimming, may rub shoulders. Such a border may form a windbreak, separate a long or irregular garden into smaller units or provide shelter and backdrops for other, lower plantings.

It is in any combination of these roles, and in company with bulbs, perennials and annuals, that shrubs play a part in the sort of garden most of us labour over. This is the garden that bursts into glory with the beginning of spring, but it is also the summer garden and the fall garden — and the garden where such perennial weeds as couch grass and goutweed must be battled if it is to survive and fulfil the gardener's vision for it.

Choosing and Planting Shrubs

How does one get started? Slowly. Good gardens evolve gradually; they do not spring up overnight. So relax and enjoy the garden-making experience. First, do a little homework:
• Browse through books and catalogues, visit gardens to look at shrubs, and learn how one differs from another; discover what you really like.
• Know your own garden. Is the soil heavy or light, acidic or alkaline? Is the site sunny or shady, sheltered or bleak? What is your hardiness zone?
• Try to visualize the mature size and shape of a shrub. How will it look in the chosen spot in five years' time? Shrubs come in all shapes and sizes – short and dumpy, tall and slender, dense or sparse, erect or droopy. A little detective work can uncover the perfect one for each gardener's needs.
• Think beyond the display of spring bloom, which can be short-lived. Does the shrub have attractive foliage or good bark for winter interest? Will it have fall colour or fruits?

Choosing shrubs becomes a matter of matching a plant's requirements with personal preferences and available garden spaces. It is rather like fitting together a jigsaw puzzle. The main pitfall to avoid is the familiar headlong rush into the garden centre on the first warm spring day without a clue as to what one would like or where it will go. Spring fever leads to expensive mistakes and wasted effort.

Shrubs are sold bare root, balled and burlapped or container-grown. Bare-root plants are usually dug in late fall and held in cold storage over winter, ready for early spring sale. The roots are wrapped in some form of damp packaging and sealed in plastic to keep them moist. These are commonly sold at chain stores, supermarkets and other nongarden stores. Look for plants with clean, healthy-looking bark and firm buds. Reject plants with new growth already starting; it means they have broken dormancy, a sign of improper storage. Nurseries that grow their own stock will sell dormant bare-root plants, dug directly from the nursery row, in early spring. Take along some wet burlap to protect the roots on the trip home. It is vital to keep the roots moist.

Plant bare-root stock as soon after purchase as possible. If more than a couple of days must elapse, check that the packaging is moist and hold the plants in a shady spot. If planting cannot be done for several days, remove the packaging and "heel-in" the shrub in a shady spot. To do this, dig a V-shaped trench, lay the branches up against one side of the trench and cover the roots with soil. Water well. Plant properly as soon as possible.

"Balled and burlapped" means the plant is dug with a large rootball of earth that is wrapped with burlap and tied to hold it securely in place. This method is mainly reserved for trees and evergreen shrubs, but deciduous plants are sometimes shipped this way (magnolias and rhododendrons should always be). If planting is delayed, keep the shrub in the shade and make sure the rootball is moist. When planting, put the plant into the prepared hole with the burlap intact. Cut the string, and roll the burlap down around the rootball. No burlap should be showing when planting is completed; any piece sticking out of the soil will act as a wick and rob the surrounding soil of moisture.

Bare-root and balled-and-burlapped stock is the most common, but another option remains. Container-grown plants extend the planting season. They can be removed from their containers and planted with little root damage. In theory, it is possible to plant them at any time during the growing season, but in practice, I would avoid planting during a hot, dry spell. Water the pot thoroughly before planting. 69

Metal or plastic containers must be removed. Papier-mâché pots can be left intact, but slash several cuts in the sides to let the roots escape and break off the pot rim below soil level to avoid the wick effect. Or remove the pot entirely.

Refuse to buy newly potted container plants. The root system should be well established at time of sale if the shrub is to transplant easily. The roots will be visible through the drainage holes in the base of the pot. Conversely, root-bound plants are a bad buy. To find out if they are, it is necessary to remove the pot – never be shy about asking to examine the root system of a container-grown plant. Any strong roots encircling the rootball in the pot

Long-term investments, shrubs such as Pieris japonica *are very rewarding.*

will continue to grow in this way after planting and can eventually strangle the growing shrub or tree.

Shrubs, once planted, will be around for many years; therefore, it is worthwhile doing the job properly. The rules of planting are few and boil down to plain common sense.

Dig the hole with enthusiasm, keeping the top layer of good soil separate from the poorer subsoil. Remove all large stones or builders' rubbish, and amend the soil where necessary. Add sand to heavy clay

soils and humus to light sandy ones. In fact, humus will help any soil.

The hole must be big enough to spread the plant roots out naturally, with at least six inches to spare beyond the roots. Make it deep enough to allow planting to the same depth at which the shrub was previously growing. A cane laid across the hole will help to match the old soil mark with the new planting.

Using sharp pruners, trim off any badly damaged or bruised roots, and gently spread the roots out in their natural position. Refill the hole, leaving the pile of topsoil to go in last. Gently work some soil around the roots as the filling-in progresses to avoid leaving air pockets. I find a piece of 2-by-4 scrap lumber useful for tamping the soil down into place to start with. When the hole is half full, tread the soil down firmly with your boot. Repeat the firming-down to finish the job, but do not fill the planting hole completely. Leave a slight hollow, and form a little moat around the shrub with the remaining soil to hold water.

Ongoing Care

Water well, making sure the entire planting area is soaked. Until the shrub is established, the soaking should be repeated weekly during dry weather. Lack of proper watering is the major cause of death in newly planted trees and shrubs. You have been warned.

If the weather is hot and sunny, it will be of benefit to rig some form of shading over newly planted shrubs. Something as simple as a length of snow fencing or burlap draped over a framework of tomato stakes will do the trick.

The thought of actually cutting pieces off live plants seems to throw some people into a tizzy. The majority of spring-flowering shrubs need little pruning for several years. Only forsythia and honeysuckle are vigorous enough to need pruning on a regular basis. Here, simply cut out one or two of the oldest shoots as soon as the flowers are finished. This will encourage new growth from the base, which will produce flowers the following season. Diseased or damaged wood on any species should be removed as soon as it is noticed.

In the following list of shrubs are plants I have chosen from my own "book of experience" to enhance the spring garden with colour and fragrance. They are relatively easy to come by and to care for, and even after flowering, their presence will add to the charm of the garden as it goes through the ensuing seasons.

Amelanchier spp

(serviceberry)

Amelanchiers can be large shrubs or small trees and are known under an assortment of common names, including serviceberry, sarviceberry, Juneberry, shadbush, shadblow, Saskatoon berry and snowy mespilus. Flowering in early spring before the leaves unfurl, the plant takes on a lacy, billowy appearance. If the weather turns warm, the display may last only a few days, but it is pure enchantment. In her *Wood and Garden* (1899), the incomparable Gertrude Jekyll wrote: "The snowy mespilus shows like puffs of smoke among the firs and birches, full of its milk-white, cherrylike bloom — a true woodland shrub or small tree." All thrive in ordinary garden soil and need a sunny or lightly shaded position. Little pruning is necessary.

Hardy to zone 4, shadblow (*Amelanchier canadensis*) is a most attractive small tree; the fall foliage is brilliant yellow, sometimes with sprinklings of orange and red. The fruit is black, juicy and sweet. It is native to Canada only in Nova Scotia but occurs in bogs and swamps from Maine to South Carolina. Shadblow is a natural for wet areas in the garden.

Amelanchier alnifolia, Saskatoon berry or serviceberry, is a very hardy (zone 1) native of the Great Plains from Manitoba and Saskatchewan to Nebraska. Plains Indians mixed the fruit with buffalo meat and fat to make the pemmican that sustained them through the long winter. The plant has now been developed for commercial fruit production, and a number of named selections with superior fruit qualities are listed in nursery catalogues. 'Honeywood' and 'Smoky' are the most widely available.

Chaenomeles spp

(flowering quince)

Botanists appear to delight in reclassifying plants, so *Chaenomeles* may be better known to some people as *Cydonia* or *japonica*. Under whatever name it is found, the flowering quince will provide a brilliant patch of colour in early spring. The flowers can be red, pink or white and either single or double. Sporadic flowers may appear in late spring and again in fall, but they do not compare with the early spring display. Newly emerging foliage is red-bronze, and then it turns a glossy dark green that it retains until the leaves fall. Branches sagging under the weight of fragrant greenish yellow fruit more than compensate for any lack of fall colour in the foliage. When fully ripe, the fruit 71 makes delicious preserves, a fact more commonly taken advantage of in England than in North America.

The shrubs will thrive in ordinary garden loam in the sun, but they can be thorny, so avoid planting close to walkways. They are especially attractive when trained against a wall. Bushes need little pruning except for an occasional thinning of overcrowded branches after flowering. Wall-trained plants are pruned by cutting back the previous season's growth to two or three buds after flowering.

Propagation can be done by layering branches in autumn, removing suckers from the base of established bushes or taking cuttings of firm young shoots in the summer. Rabbits are partial to flowering quince, and overwinter damage can be severe. Having a young plant or two in reserve makes good sense if the furry critters reside in your locality.

Flowering quince is generally listed as hardy to zone 5b, but many forms will survive and flower in protected sites in zone 5a, especially where good snow cover is normal. It is not possible, of course, to rely on such protection for wall-trained forms. There are so many named cultivars that

listing them all is impossible. Checking local nurseries and gardens is the best way of finding out what is available and what does well in any particular area.

Cornus spp

(dogwood)

Although very limited in where it will survive, *Cornus florida*, flowering dogwood, is so much a part of the spring scene that I feel it must be included. If grown in full sun, rather than in a woodland setting, it forms a bushy tree that could be called a large shrub, branched to the ground and often multi-trunked. In the filtered sun of the woodland, it becomes a tall, slender, graceful tree that flowers more sparsely.

The showy white "petals" of dogwood are really bracts or modified leaves surrounding the true flower, a flat cluster of tiny insignificant blooms. As a bonus, the leaves turn deep red early in the fall. Clusters of shiny bright red berries will carry the dogwood's ornamental value through to Christmas if the birds do not strip it first.

Given a well-drained soil, dogwoods are easy to grow once they become established. They do have a reputation for being difficult to transplant, however, so buy only balled-and-burlapped or pot-grown plants.

There are many named selections, some of which have pink or red flowers. Hardiness will vary even within a variety, and the wise gardener will ask the nurseryman where the plants originated. Propagating material collected from northern plants will produce hardier stock than material collected from southern ones. In general, they can be expected to survive down to zone 6b.

Cornus mas, cornelian cherry, is hardier, and plants are surviving, if not thriving, in Ottawa; officially, it is hardy to zone 5b. This shrub flowers in very early spring, long before the forsythia for which it can be mistaken from a distance. It will grow up to 20 feet tall under good conditions.

Corylus spp

(hazel)

Hazel twigs make the world's best supports for peas and, if space allows, are worth growing for this reason alone. I have vivid childhood memories of nervously leading an apparently monstrous horse and cart down a country lane to pick up bundles of pea sticks (corylus twigs). Alas, I now use wire netting to support the peas, but I still watch for the swelling and opening of the hazel catkins to tell me winter has finally lost its grip and is giving way to spring.

The hazels are large shrubs for full sun or light shade that thrive in any well-drained soil. Little maintenance is necessary, apart from occasional pruning to keep the plant within bounds.

Corylus avellana, European hazel or filbert (zone 5), provides winter interest with its dainty catkins hanging along the bare branches. It is very beautiful when they burst into soft yellow bloom. The foliage that follows is dark to medium green with an interesting texture. I have seen it described as coarse but personally find it attractive. The nuts add summer interest with their distinctive husks that resemble tiny helmets, and they are delicious if you can beat the squirrels to them.

Corylus avellana 'Contorta,' twisted hazel or Harry Lauder's walking stick (zone 5), was discovered in a hedgerow in Gloucestershire, England, around 1863. I have not seen it grow more than 6 feet tall. With its strangely twisted stems and puckered leaves, it is popular as an accent shrub and the branches are much sought after for flower arrangements.

Corylus maxima 'Purpurea,' giant filbert, is a shrub or small tree valued for its fruit. It has deep purple foliage that turns green later in the summer. It is hardy only to zone 6.

Daphne spp

(daphne)

Daphnes are small, attractive shrubs that bloom in early spring and are valued for the fragrance of their flowers. The name is believed to commemorate Daphne, daughter of the river god of Greek mythology. According to legend, she was

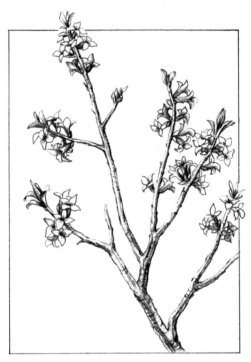

turned into a tree to save her from pursuit by Apollo.

Perfect drainage and a relatively cool root run are recommended for success with daphnes; a loose sandy soil with a reasonably reliable water supply would be ideal. Although a somewhat alkaline soil is preferable, researchers have found that these shrubs are not as insistent on a ready supply of lime as older texts would have us believe.

Daphnes are not easy to transplant unless they are container-grown, and even then, small plants move best. Bare-root plants are not a good buy. Self-sown seedlings will sometimes appear near an established plant. These should be moved to new quarters when quite small to reduce root disturbance as much as possible. Take a good clump of soil with the roots. They do not need much pruning.

Daphne mezereum, known as February daphne (zone 3), was introduced from Europe in colonial days and has now naturalized in some areas of Canada, particularly in Nova Scotia, and in the northeastern

United States. It is the earliest shrub to flower here in Ottawa (but in early April rather than February). The previous year's stems are wreathed in clusters of purple-pink, intensely fragrant flowers before the foliage opens. Coming at the end of our Canadian winter, it is indeed a welcome sight, and in the summer, attractive scarlet berries cover the branches. Both berries and foliage are poisonous. There is a white form with creamy white flowers and yellow berries. Selections of the white form, 'Paul's White' and 'Bowles' White,' have pure white flowers.

Daphne burkwoodii, Burkwood's daphne (zone 5), is a lovely semievergreen hybrid bred in the 1930s. It carries small, leafy heads of fragrant, soft pink, star-shaped flowers in May and June. Sparse flowers may also be produced throughout the summer and fall. This daphne grows into a dense, broad, mounded form 3 to 5 feet tall and is well suited to small gardens.

Daphne cneorum, garland flower, is an evergreen trailing shrub with a spreading habit some 6 to 12 inches high and 2 to 3 feet wide. It can be temperamental, but the masses of rich pink blossoms that waft their heady scent about the garden are well worth the effort needed to get it established. In the right spot, it is a good plant for the rock garden or as a ground cover. Hardy to zone 2b, it needs snow cover on the prairies.

Erica spp

(heath)

Anyone who has visited or seen photographs of Alan Bloom's heath garden at Bressingham, England, cannot doubt the beauty of these plants. Heaths, in general, need a well-drained, but not excessively dry, peaty acidic soil and full sun to light shade. If such conditions can be met, the plants will give little trouble.

Erica carnea, spring heath, is a ground-hugging evergreen shrub growing to 12 inches tall. In early spring, the flowers, in

Erica darleyensis is known as winter heath because of its flowering time in mild climates. Here, of course, it blooms in early spring. The deep pink 'George Rendall' and the white 'Silberschmelze' ('Molten Silver') are the easiest to find. The latter hybrid seems to be slightly tougher than spring heath.

Forsythia spp

(golden bells)

Forsythia is a plant that, like chrysanthemum and poinsettia, is more widely known by the Latin name than by its common name of golden bells. Masses of bright yellow flowers blooming before the foliage opens make this well-loved shrub a fine harbinger of spring.

Forsythia was named in honour of a Scotsman, William Forsyth, the king's gardener at the royal palace of Kensington, in England. A wily, controversial figure, Forsyth concocted a mixture called Forsyth's plaister, which he claimed would cure any defects in growing trees, including restoring to health oaks where nothing but the bark remained – quite a claim, even for the 18th century. The mix-

white, pinks and reds, begin to provide a solid mass of colour that can last for weeks if varieties are carefully chosen for succession of bloom. The correct name is now *Erica herbacea*, but it will be some time before nursery catalogues catch up with the reclassification.

Although they are generally hardy to zone 6, I have grown several in zone 5 and found they came through most winters well, providing there was good snow cover. They are more shade- and lime-tolerant than I would have expected, growing happily in a raised bed of peaty soil over limestone, up against a north-facing wall. The varieties 'King George' (deep pink), 'Springwood Pink,' 'Springwood White,' 'Vivellii' (carmine) and 'Winter Beauty' (bright pink) are the most widely available of almost 50 named forms.

ture, made of lime, dung, wood ashes, soapsuds, sand, urine and so on, was later discredited, but a gullible British government in desperate need of timber during the Napoleonic wars paid Forsyth a generous gratuity of £1,500.

For many Canadian gardens, older varieties of forsythia have one serious drawback. Although the plants are quite hardy, the flower buds are killed by temperatures below about minus 20 degrees F. Most springs will see flowers at the base of the plant only, below the snow line. Three new introductions from the Central Experimental Farm in Ottawa have changed that. First was the variety 'Ottawa,' a chance seedling in a row of *Forsythia ovata* plants, which has buds that are hardy to about minus 30 degrees, so most winters, it will flower to the top in zone 5.

That discovery led to a breeding program which has given rise to 'Northern Gold,' with flowers hardy to zone 4 and even to zone 3 in many winters. Both are tall shrubs, growing 7 to 8 feet high. 'Happy Centennial,' the latest introduction, is a low (2-foot) ground cover, hardy to zone 4 and beyond where there is reliable snow cover.

Several hardy new varieties have also been introduced in the United States in recent years – among them 'Meadowlark,' 'Vermont Sun' and 'Northern Sun' – but none seem to be available in Canada yet.

Genista spp

(broom)

I cannot understand why brooms are not planted more frequently in gardens. They are hardy shrubs that will thrive in full sun and the type of dry, sandy soils normally considered difficult. Even in such poor conditions, they make a lovely showing of golden, pealike flowers in mid-to-late spring.

Genista tinctoria, dyer's greenweed or woadwaxen (zone 3), has for centuries been valued for the yellow dye it yields.

The stem fibres were also used to make a coarse cloth. Governor John Endecott of Salem, Massachusetts, is credited with introducing it to North America around 1630. Growing to 3 feet, 'Royal Gold' is the selection most readily available.

My favourite, *Genista tinctoria* 'Plena,' is harder to find but well worth the search. It is a dwarf form with double flowers that hugs the ground and looks wonderful with the mauve ornamental onion *Allium ostrowskianum* growing up through it.

Genista pilosa, silkyleaf woadwaxen (zone 5), which grows about a foot high, makes an ideal ground cover on poor, sandy soils. 'Vancouver Gold' is a selection recently introduced by the University of British Columbia.

Kalmia spp

(American laurel)

Kalmia latifolia, mountain laurel (zone 5b), is a slow-growing evergreen shrub native to eastern North America. The large clusters of bowl-shaped blossoms are

Jaynes at the Connecticut Agricultural Experimental Station, and many of the new hybrids are beginning to appear in nursery catalogues.

Kalmia angustifolia, known as sheep laurel, is a small native shrub, hardy to zone 1, that is not nearly as fussy about its soil as is *K. latifolia*. Unfortunately, its beauty cannot compare with that of the mountain laurel; the flowers cluster around the stem rather than on the ends of the branches.

Lonicera spp

(honeysuckle)

beautiful and, to my eyes, rival any rhododendron. Flower colour varies from white through the range of pinks to red, and usually the closed buds hold the deepest colour, opening to a paler shade. The leathery leaves are toxic to cattle and sheep.

A fibrous root system makes mountain laurel easy to transplant, but it is choosy about soil type. It will languish and fade away if not planted in a cool, moist but well-drained acidic soil. Cultivation around the shallow roots should be avoided. A mulch of pine needles will help to promote acidity, keep the soil moist and prevent weeds. It will grow in sun or shade, but flowering will be reduced somewhat by shade.

Difficult to propagate, kalmias are not popular with nurserymen, so availability varies from one area to another. As some are now being propagated by tissue culture, the situation should improve. A great deal of breeding work has been done in recent years, especially by Dr. Richard

Honeysuckles are well enough known to need no introduction. There are around 150 species, some of which are among the best flowering shrubs for the colder areas of Canada. Most like a sunny position in average garden soil, and they are easily propagated from seeds or cuttings.

Lonicera tatarica, Tatarian honeysuckle, is extremely hardy (zone 2) and can grow 10 to 12 feet tall, taking on the appearance of a small multistemmed tree. Depending on variety, the late-spring flowers are white to pink or rose-red, followed by red or yellow berries in middle to late summer.

Two other spring-flowering honeysuck- 77

les are widely available, both of them suitable for hedging. If kept closely trimmed, they will not flower and fruit as freely, but where space allows, they can be grown as informal hedges, requiring only that branches growing out of line be cut back. *Lonicera korolkowii zabelii*, Zabel's honeysuckle (zone 2b), has red flowers followed by red berries. It grows up to 6 feet tall but can be kept to half this height as a formal hedge. As a specimen shrub, it is outstanding. 'Clavey's Dwarf' honeysuckle (*L. xylosteoides*) is the result of a cross between the Tatarian and the European fly honeysuckles. Because of the latter parent, it is not as hardy, surviving down to zone 5 only. It grows 3 feet tall and has cream-coloured flowers and large red fruit. Its size makes it especially useful as a low hedge or foundation planting.

Magnolia spp

(magnolia)

Magnolias have a reputation for being difficult, yet some of the very best specimens are found in old abandoned gardens where they have had to fend for themselves for decades. They are also generally thought of as trees and shrubs for the South, but some of the hardier ones will certainly grow as far north as Ottawa. I strongly suspect that more magnolias succumb to the constant interference of busy gardeners than are killed by the weather.

The time to plant a magnolia is when it is in flower. This may sound like strange advice, but they have brittle, fleshy roots that tend to break during planting. If the plant is actively growing, the injury will heal, but when the magnolia is not in active growth, a rot can set in that will eventually kill the shrub. For the same reason, they resent a gardener grubbing around in their root zone; once planted, they like to be left severely alone. They are definitely not shrubs for underplanting with annual bedding plants.

A site in full sun is best, but they will take light shade. A good, deep, moist, acidic soil suits them. In colder areas where late-spring frost is common, a northern exposure can reduce frost damage by delaying flowering.

Magnolia stellata, star magnolia (zone 5), is number one among the hardy magnolias for the home garden. It is one of the earliest to flower, and the starry white or pink flowers are perfumed. It is enchanting underplanted with a sea of massed blue grape hyacinths. Plant them around the perimeter of the shrub's roots, and let them self-seed to fill in. A mature specimen can be 15 to 20 feet tall, but it is slow-growing and carries flowers even as a young plant. Named cultivars are available, of which 'Royal Star,' with larger flowers, is among the hardiest. 'Waterlily,' with pink buds opening to white, is noted as highly fragrant.

Magnolia soulangiana, or saucer magnolia, is generally listed as hardy to zone 5b, but there are several large specimens in the Ottawa area (zone 5). The pinkish white flowers can be as wide as 6 inches. Buds may be damaged by frosts following a warm spell, but winter cold does not harm them. This magnolia can grow into a large plant, as tall as 20 feet, so allow plenty of room at planting time.

Mahonia spp

(Oregon grape)

Of the hundred or so species of *Mahonia*, a few are native to North America and have been popular in our gardens for a long time. Thomas Nuttall named these handsome evergreen shrubs in his *Genera of American Plants* (1818) to honour Bernard McMahon, a prominent Philadelphia nurseryman and author of *The American Gardener's Calendar* (1806), a book that went through 11 editions by 1857 (and a title change: *McMahon's American Gardener*) and still has relevance today.

Mahonia aquifolium, Oregon grape (zone 5), occurs naturally in the Pacific Northwest and is Oregon's state flower. I first made its acquaintance, however, at Burghley House, the stately home of the Marquis of Exeter, in Lincolnshire, England. A lowly undergardener at the time, I was hoeing in the shrubberies and was attracted by the glossy leaves. The plant has remained a firm favourite of mine.

It is a shrub for all seasons, with something to offer throughout the year. In spring, the new leaves unfold to a pale reddish bronze, changing to light, glossy yellow-green and then to a shiny dark green as summer progresses. With the coming of fall, the leaves turn a purplish brown. Large terminal clusters of vivid yellow, slightly scented flowers are carried throughout the spring. These are followed by bluish black berries with a whitish bloom that resemble grapes. The hollylike foliage is greatly valued by flower arrangers and is one of the most reliable for preserving for winter use. Whole sprays, as well as individual twigs, can be cut and stood in glycerin. The species itself is the most readily available, but new selections such as 'Woodland King' are beginning to appear.

Oregon grape seems to do well in most

soils and in either sun or shade, but it prefers partial shade. The evergreen foliage will turn brown when exposed to winter wind and sun, and some spring pruning is necessary; but it quickly recovers its attractiveness when new spring growth starts. In colder areas, shade from winter sun and shelter are recommended, and good snow cover will reduce damage. Usually growing 3 to 6 feet tall, it can reach 9 feet where conditions are favourable.

Mahonia repens, creeping mahonia (zone 3), is a low (10-inch) ground cover. The leaves are dull blue-green in summer, turning to a rich purple later. Yellow flowers in April produce the typical grapelike fruits in August or September. This species spreads slowly by underground runners and makes a good ground cover.

Pieris spp

(pieris)

Pieris (zone 5b) consists of upright evergreen shrubs of neat habit, with stiff 79

spreading branches and dense rosettelike foliage. Pendulous clusters of waxy flowers, which have a light fragrance, open in early spring and last two or three weeks. In England, they are commonly called lily-of-the-valley shrubs, and I remember being fascinated as a child to find what I thought were lily-of-the-valley flowers growing on a shrub. New growth is a rich bronze turning to a lustrous dark green, and the dormant flower buds, which are reddish, add a bit of winter interest.

A well-drained but moist acidic soil is preferred, and pieris will appreciate having lots of peat moss or other organic matter worked into the bed before planting. They do well in full sun or partial shade but should have shelter from strong winds. Pieris grow slowly, reaching perhaps 6 feet in eight years or so, but they eventually make excellent large specimen shrubs. In the north, they can suffer badly from dehydration caused by winter sun and wind and will fare better in the shelter of other evergreens.

Prune only to remove dead wood or occasionally to lightly shape the bush. Deadheading, removing the flower heads as soon as the blooms fade, will help to promote the next year's flower display. For this reason, it is well worth forgoing the dubious pleasure of seeing rather insignificant fruits ripen to a dull brown.

A number of cultivars have been selected and named, but availability is limited. Three popular ones in Canada are 'Mountain Fire,' with white flowers and bright red new foliage; 'Valley Rose,' with pastel pink flowers and dark green foliage; and 'Variegata,' with white flowers and narrow white margins on the leaves.

Prunus spp

(cherry, almond)

Prunus comprises a very large group of shrubs and small trees, including cherries, plums and flowering almonds. Many of the white-flowering native shrubs seen in hedgerows belong to the genus. As well as being spring-flowering, they help attract fruit-eating birds into the garden.

Prunus cistena, purple-leaved sand cherry (zone 4), is one of the best coloured-foliage shrubs. It keeps its purple tone all summer. The white flowers appear with the opening leaves and are not very visible from a distance. Close up, however, they make a delightful contrast. I especially like them underplanted with self-sown forget-me-nots.

A vigorous shrub that will reach 8 feet in height when grown in rich soil, it can occasionally be cut back almost to ground level to rejuvenate the plant. The fruit are small, dark purple cherries that are hard to see against the leaves, although the birds always manage to find them.

Prunus tomentosa is called Nanking or Manchu cherry. It is a very hardy plant (zone 2) that can be grown as an individual specimen or trimmed as a hedge. If allowed to grow, it can reach 10 feet in height, but I kept a row of them trimmed back to a 3-foot-high formal hedge for about eight years. The flowers are a soft pink in midspring and are followed by small, bright red cherries that I find good to eat. Some authors claim they are fit only for pies and preserves, but I suspect they have never actually tasted them. There is also a form with white flowers and fruit that has a more delicate, slightly sweeter flavour. Even when I kept my Nanking cherry to a low hedge clipped three times each summer, I still got a good display of flowers and fruit inside the hedge.

Prunus triloba, flowering almond (zone 2b), is a large shrub, growing up to 15 feet tall, with bright pink flowers. The fruit of the single form should not be eaten because of its high prussic-acid content. The double-flowered form, 'Multiplex,' is sterile and much more attractive. It is also available grafted onto a 5- or 6-foot stem to form a small tree. The closely related dwarf Russian almond (*P. tenella*) grows only about 4 feet tall, but it suckers badly and can be a nuisance in a small garden.

Rhododendron spp

(rhododendron, azalea)

No discussion of spring-flowering shrubs would be complete without mentioning rhododendrons and azaleas. Their popularity persists despite their demanding requirements. Given a mild climate, a woodsy acidic soil and summer shade, these plants will prosper; without them, they become a real challenge. Many gardeners, however, thrive on challenge.

Most of the readily available rhododendrons are hardy to zone 6, some will grow in zone 5, and a few will tough it out in zone 4 – provided they have the conditions they require, which I described above. Even so, many of the hardy broad-leaved rhododendrons suffer so much winter injury that they become merely sticks with tufts of leaves on top. This rather sad state of affairs may continue until a so-called "test" winter kills the plants. Many otherwise sane people still consider it worthwhile for the display of flowers in May.

There is one small-leaved rhododendron that does seem to survive against all odds, keeps its leaves and covers itself with blooms each spring. It also has more charm than the average rhododendron. 'P.J. Mezzitt' (usually listed as P.J.M.) does not have the gigantic flower heads that most people associate with rhododendrons. Its mauve-pink flowers are not in large terminal clusters but are scattered down the branches. It is hardy to zone 4 and has survived minus 40 degrees F in my garden and still bloomed profusely. It makes a delightful backdrop to daffodils. The foliage turns a lovely plum colour in 81 the fall and greens up again in spring.

In general, the difference between rhododendrons and azaleas is that the latter lose their leaves (there are, however, some evergreen azaleas as well). In areas with marginal growing conditions, azaleas seem to survive better and flower more regularly than rhododendrons. I grew both for several years but gradually swung over to mainly azaleas. Because they put out new leaves each spring, they escape the winter-damaged foliage that disfigures rhododendrons. Many azaleas are sweetly scented; the variety 'Narcissiflora' is a particular favourite of mine.

Ribes spp

(currant)

The name *Ribes* is thought to have derived from the Arabic or Persian word ribas, which means acid-tasting. Anyone who has picked and eaten gooseberries or black currants, both members of this tribe, will agree with the name. There are some 150 different *Ribes*, but only the ones known generally as flowering currants are

of interest for the ornamental garden.

Ribes odoratum, known as clove or buffalo currant, is a plant I covet for my new shrub-garden-in-the-making. It was collected in Missouri by Lewis and Clark, and by 1812, cuttings to be planted at Monticello had already reached Thomas Jefferson.

Though not the most handsome of bushes, its spring display of flowers, which perfume the air with a spicy clovelike scent, more than makes up for any lack of good shape or form. The showy yellow flowers, which fall in drooping clusters 1½ to 2 inches long, are beloved by bees. If you can beat the birds to it, the fruit is black and edible. Apparently, the foliage, which is attractive during the summer, turns to glowing scarlet in fall, but I have not as yet seen the plant in fall plumage.

Clove currant will do well in any average soil and is tolerant of sun or shade. It could be a good spring-flowering shrub for problem areas. Claude Barr, who spent his lifetime studying native plants of the American plains, wrote that it "will grow and perform well in drier and more difficult gardening situations than perhaps any other fruit bearer." He also noted that it reached a height of some 40 inches on the arid plains. In the less hostile environment of an average garden, it can grow to 8 feet tall. It is hardy to zone 2.

Equally hardy, *Ribes aureum*, golden currant, is similar to and often confused with *R. odoratum*, although the flowers lack some of the pervasive spiciness of the clove currant.

Ribes alpinum, alpine currant, is less spectacular, but it can be trimmed to form a good small hedge. The greenish yellow flowers are followed by juicy but inedible scarlet berries. It also is hardy to zone 2.

Salix spp

(willow)

Like the catkins on hazel, the "pussies" on willow are a sure sign that winter is

available in nurseries. The spring display of catkins and the curiously flattened branches are prized by flower arrangers.

Sambucus spp

(elder)

There are two elders that bloom early enough to be classed as spring-flowering: *Sambucus pubens*, the native scarlet elder, and *S. racemosa*, the European red elder. The golden-leaved forms of the latter species would earn themselves a place in my garden no matter when they flowered.

Sambucus racemosa 'Plumosa Aurea,' the golden plume red elder, has deeply cut, golden foliage that is pale yellow as it opens and turns more golden as it matures. The form 'Sutherland Golden,' which originated in Sutherland, Saskatchewan, has even brighter leaves that keep their colour all summer.

losing its grip. The site for willows must be chosen with care, as their roots are notorious for plugging drains and tile beds. They will grow in average garden soil but are naturals for a wet, boggy corner of the garden.

Willows have male and female flowers on different plants. Both sexes have "pussies," but those on the male plants open to release the yellow pollen and are more attractive, unless you have pollen allergies.

Salix caprea, goat willow, from Europe, has larger and showier catkins than the native pussy willow (*S. discolor*), but it is hardy only to zone 5 rather than zone 2. Both make large shrubs, eventually reaching about 15 feet. It is advisable to cut the shrubs back hard every two or three years and burn or dispose of the stems to minimize the many pests and diseases that can attack willows. This also helps to keep the shrub down to a reasonable size.

Salix sachalinensis 'Sekka,' Japanese fan-tailed willow (zone 3), is occasionally

Both are tall shrubs, growing to 12 feet high. Their wood is brittle, and branches may be lost in winter storms; but growth is rapid, and any damage is quickly made good. The scarlet elder is even taller and can reach 25 feet. All are hardy to zone 3.

In addition to their flowers and attractive foliage, elders are noted for their fruit, which will attract birds. The best species 83 for wine making (and my family is very partial to elderberry wine) is the European elder (*Sambucus nigra*), which has black fruit, but the above two species can also be used. The golden forms do not crop as heavily as green-leaved forms but are much more garden-worthy.

Syringa spp

(lilac)

Lilac was one of the pioneer plants, and many an old farmstead is marked by its ever-expanding clumps of common lilac and golden glow rudbeckia, in many cases the only remaining signs of habitation.

All the lilacs are hardy to zone 2b, and many to zone 2. The removal of the flowers as they fade will improve the display the following year by preventing seed formation. Any suckers growing around the base of the plant should also be removed every year. Other pruning is seldom needed until the plants become mature; then, the occasional removal of an old branch will promote young growth from the base.

84   *Syringa vulgaris*. If I had room for only one lilac in my garden, it would have to be one of these French hybrids. Just which one would depend on my feelings when I actually bought it: white for hope, purple for passion, mauve for melancholia, pink for a girl or blue for a boy? Then there is, in addition, the choice of single or double.

Syringa prestoniae. If there were space for two lilacs, my second choice would be from the group first raised by (and named after) Isabella Preston in Ottawa in the 1920s: hybrids between *S. reflexa*, nodding lilac, and *S. villosa*, late lilac. From the first parent, they derive their longer, more open flower habit, while the other parent imparts the later flowering time. The colour range is limited to pinks, mauves and pale lilac, but the habit and perfume of the flowers is distinctive.

Syringa hyacinthiflora. If I could fit in three lilacs, the third would be from the group called the American hybrids, which are crosses between *S. oblata*, early lilac, and the common lilac. Their group name derives from the appearance of the flowers, which are somewhat like those of the hyacinth. As the early-lilac parentage may indicate, they bloom just before the French hybrids but are otherwise very similar in flower form and perfume.

I would also want to plant a sample of the Japanese tree lilac (*Syringa reticulata*), although it blooms in early summer and is therefore outside the scope of this book.

Viburnum spp

(viburnum)

"Handsome and vigorous shrubs of northern regions, beautiful in berry as well as flower and, with few exceptions, of the easiest cultivation," wrote William Robinson of viburnums in *The English Flower Garden* of 1933. Time, and the introduction of several new species and cultivars, has only enhanced the plants' reputation.

The viburnums comprise a very large family of shrubs, with species that flower from midwinter (in warm regions) to early summer. They are particularly useful since they will grow and flower equally well in light shade or sun. The following are usually readily available in nurseries:

Viburnum burkwoodii, Burkwood's viburnum (zone 6), forms an upright shrub that grows to 8 feet and produces small globes of white flowers in April. They have a spicy scent and develop into fruit with little ornamental value.

Viburnum carlesii, also known as Korean spice viburnum, is one of the parents of the above species. The flower form is similar, and the blooms are clove-scented and very fragrant. It is slightly hardier, to zone 5b, and has a more rounded form.

Viburnum juddii, raised at the Arnold Arboretum in 1920, is also an offspring of the Korean spice viburnum and has a similar scent, but it inherited additional hardiness from its other parent, *V. bitchiuense*, and will survive to zone 5. It is also less subject to leaf spot than the previous two.

Viburnum farreri is named after the great British plant explorer Reginald Farrer, who found it growing wild in northern China. It was first named *V. fragrans* because of its perfume. In *On the Eaves of the World*, Farrer describes it as having "gracious arching masses, 10 feet high and more across, whose naked boughs in spring before the foliage become one blaze of soft pink lilac spikelets, breathing an intense fragrance of heliotrope." The flowers are highly perfumed and open so early in the spring that they may be damaged by late frosts in exposed gardens. The shrub is hardy to zone 5 and makes a slender bush about 8 feet high. The form 'Nanum' grows less than half this size. It is one parent of *V. bodnantense* 'Dawn,' which I remember in full flower in February at Kew, in England. Unfortunately, it is hardy only to zone 7.

Viburnum lantana, the wayfaring tree, has white, unscented flowers in flat-topped clusters in late spring. These turn into green berries that become red and eventually blue-black; often, all three colours are present at the same time. It makes a rounded shrub, hardy to zone 2, and will grow up to 10 feet tall.

Viburnum opulus, European cranberry, is another very hardy shrub (zone 2). It has flat heads of white flowers with a large, showy and sterile outside ring and a centre of smaller but fertile flowers that become clusters of bright red berries for good colour interest in early winter. It makes a rounded bush up to 10 feet tall and wide. The dwarf form 'Compactum' will grow to half the size. Another variety, 'Roseum,' has all-sterile flowers. The flower heads are globe-shaped, giving it the common name of snowball bush. 'Roseum' is often attacked by an aphid that causes the leaves to pucker and distort, the shoots to become twisted and the flower heads to fade rapidly. Weekly sprays with soap and water or insecticidal soap, from the time the leaves unfurl until the flowers fade, will prevent this.

Brenda Cole, freelance garden writer and columnist in the Ottawa region, trained as a horticulturist in England at Burghley House and the Royal Botanic Gardens at Kew. She moved to Canada in 1967.

CLIMATIC ZONE MAPS – CANADA

Lower zone numbers refer to increasingly cold areas, but there are not specific minimum temperature limits for each zone.

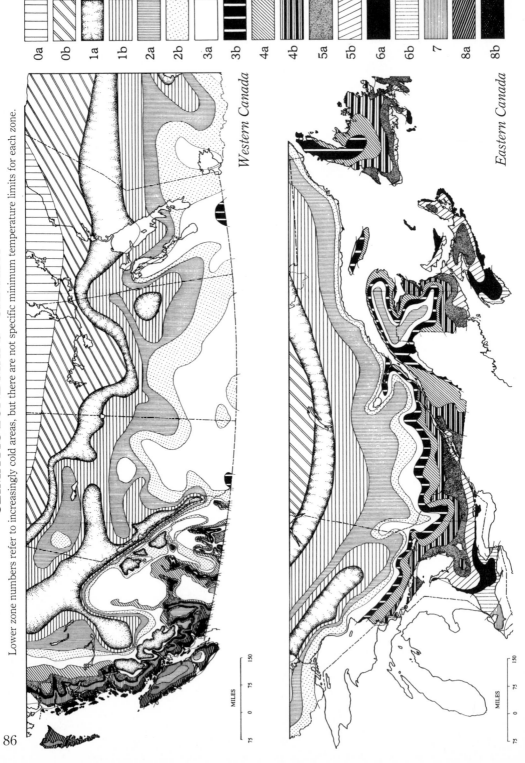

0a
0b
1a
1b
2a
2b
3a
3b
4a
4b
5a
5b
6a
6b
7
8a
8b

Western Canada

Eastern Canada

MILES
75   0   75   150

MILES
75   0   75   150

86

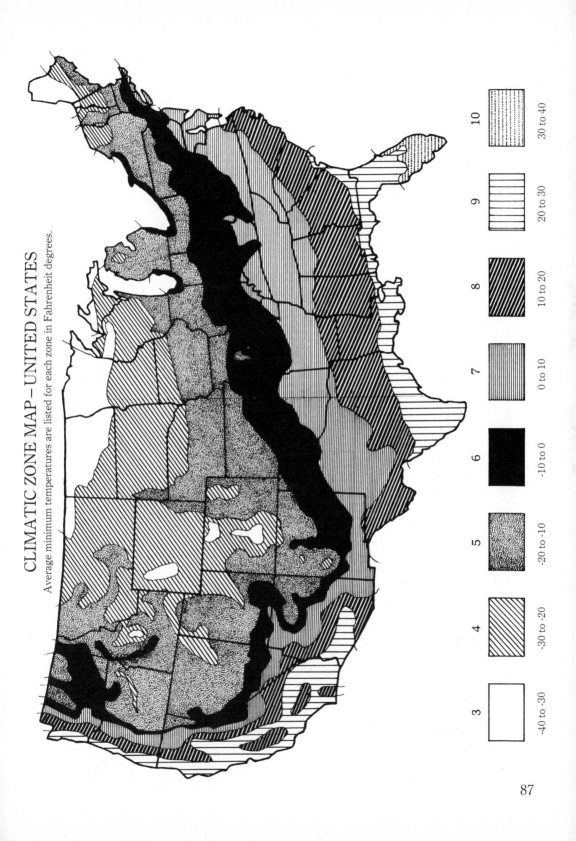

CLIMATIC ZONE MAP – UNITED STATES

Average minimum temperatures are listed for each zone in Fahrenheit degrees.

3	4	5	6	7	8	9	10
-40 to -30	-30 to -20	-20 to -10	-10 to 0	0 to 10	10 to 20	20 to 30	30 to 40

Recommended Books

Garden Design: History, Principles, Elements, Practice, by William Lake Douglas et al., Prentice Hall Canada Inc., Scarborough, Ont., 1984.

The Small Garden, by John Brookes, Macmillan, 1978.

Mail-Order Directory

It makes good sense for a gardener to check local sources of supply when starting a new garden or adding to an existing one. However, reliable mail-order sources may be able to provide unusual or challenging plants, bulbs and seeds.

It is much easier to purchase by mail within one's own country – certainly when time is a consideration – for although seeds present no problem at an international border, there are strict regulations governing importation of rooted plants and bulbs. Canadians wishing to buy from U.S. nurseries that accept foreign orders should obtain an "application form for permit to import" from The Permit Office, Plant Health Division, Agriculture Canada, Ottawa, Ontario K1A 0C6. One form is necessary for each company from which you order plants.

Imports to the United States must include an invoice showing the quantity and value of the plants, as well as a document from the Department of Agriculture certifying that the plants are disease-free.

Plants, Bulbs, Seeds

Canada

Aimers Quality Seeds & Bulbs
81 Temperance Street

Aurora, Ontario L4G 2R1
Wildflower mixtures. Price list $1.

Boughen Nurseries
Valley River Ltd.
Box 12
Valley River, Manitoba R0L 2B0
Ornamental shrubs. Catalogue free.

C.A. Cruickshank, Inc.
1015 Mount Pleasant Road
Toronto, Ontario M4P 2M1
Flowering bulbs, woodland plants, seeds.
Three catalogues (spring, midseason, fall)
$2.

Dominion Seed House
115 Guelph Street
Georgetown, Ontario L7G 4A2
Seeds, spring-flowering bulbs. Catalogue
free, to Canada only.

Farleigh Lake Gardens
Box 128
Penticton, British Columbia V2A 6J9
Perennial flowers to British Columbia, Al-
berta and Saskatchewan only. Price list
free.

Gardenimport Inc.
Box 760
Thornhill, Ontario L3T 4A5
Flowering bulbs, woodland plants, ferns.
Catalogue $2 for two years (includes four
catalogues).

Hopestead Gardens
RR 4, 6605 Hopedale Road
Sardis, British Columbia V0X 1Y0
Hardy perennial flowers. Price list free.

Hortico, Inc.
RR 1
Waterdown, Ontario L0R 2H0
Ferns, ground covers. Price list free.

McFayden Seed Co. Ltd.
Box 1800
Brandon, Manitoba R7A 6N4

Seeds, bulbs, hardy perennials, ferns,
flowering shrubs. Catalogue $2.

McMath's Daffodils
6340 Francis Road
Richmond, British Columbia V7C 1K5
Specialists in daffodils and other narcissi.
Canadian orders only. Price list free.

McMillen's Iris Garden
RR 1
Norwich, Ontario N0J 1P0
Dwarf irises a specialty. Catalogue $1.

Sears McConnell Nurseries
RR 1
Port Burwell, Ontario N0J 1T0
Flowering shrubs, perennial flowers.
Catalogue free, available also from Sears
outlets.

Stirling Perennials
RR 1
Morpeth, Ontario N0P 1X0
Hardy perennials. Catalogue $1.

Woodland Nursery
2151 Camilla Road
Mississauga, Ontario L5A 2K1
Spring-flowering shrubs; specialists in
azaleas and hardy rhododendrons. Prices
on enquiry, descriptive booklet $3.50.
Minimum order $50.

United States

Bluestone Perennials
7211 Middle Ridge Road
Madison, Ohio 44057
A large selection of perennial plants. Catalogue free.

W. Atlee Burpee & Co.
300 Park Avenue
Warminster, Pennsylvania 18974
Seed specialists, also perennial plants,
bulbs. Catalogue free.

Carroll Gardens, Inc.

Box 310
Westminster, Maryland 21157
Wildflowers, ferns, bulbs, perennials, shrubs. Catalogue $2 (U.S.).

The Cummins Garden
22 Robertsville Road
Marlboro, New Jersey 07746
Rhododendrons and azaleas, other flowering shrubs. Catalogue $1 (U.S.) refundable with order.

Far North Gardens
Dept. AG
16785 Harrison
Livonia, Michigan 48154
Seeds; wildflowers; primroses a specialty. Catalogue $2 (U.S.) for a three-year subscription.

Greer Gardens
1280 Goodpasture Island Road
Eugene, Oregon 97401
Specialists in rhododendrons and azaleas. Catalogue $2 (U.S.).

J.L. Hudson, Seedsman
Box 1058
Redwood City, California 94064
Seeds from around the world. Catalogue $1 (U.S.).

Maver Seed
Route 2, Box 265B
Asheville, North Carolina 28805
Seeds only. Perennial list $3 (U.S.); shrub list $1 (U.S.).

Milaeger's Gardens
4838 Douglas Avenue
Racine, Wisconsin 53402-2498
Perennial plants. Catalogue $1 (U.S.).

Park Seed Co.
Box 31, Cokesbury Road
Greenwood, South Carolina 29674-0001
Seeds only. Catalogue free.

Rocknoll Nursery
9210 U.S. 50
Hillsboro, Ohio 45133
Native American plants and wildflowers, dwarf and species iris, primulas, flowering rock plants, flowering shrubs, perennials. Seed list. Catalogue 44 cents in U.S. stamps or 50 cents in currency.

Roslyn Nursery
Department G
211 Burrs Lane
Dix Hills, New York 11746
Rhododendrons and azaleas, ferns, flowering shrubs, wildflowers, perennials. Catalogue $2 (U.S.).

Thompson & Morgan, Inc.
Box 1308
Jackson, New Jersey 08527
Seeds only. Catalogue free.

White Flower Farm
Litchfield, Connecticut 06759
Perennial plants shipped within continental U.S. only. Catalogue $5 (covering spring and fall issues).

Index

Credits